By the author

*The Necrofiles*

# the necrofiles II

## Donna Lypchuk

INSOMNIAC PRESS

Edited by Bill Reynolds.
Copy edited by Noelle Zitzer.
Designed by Mike O'Connor

**Canadian Cataloguing in Publication Data**

Lypchuk, Donna, 1960-
  The necrofiles II

ISBN 1-895837-53-7

1. Popular culture — Humor.  2. Canadian wit and humor (English).*  I. Title.  II. Title:Necrofiles two.

PS8573.Y63N4 1999    C818'.5402    C99-931682-6
PR9199.3.L98N4 1999

The publisher gratefully acknowledges the support of the Canada Council and the Ontario Arts Council.

Printed and bound in Canada

Insomniac Press, 393 Shaw Street,
Toronto, Ontario, Canada, M6J 2X4
www.insomniacpress.com

*To the dearly departed...*

The author would like to acknowledge the assistance and
support of the editorial staff past and present at *eye* magazine
for the past ten years.

# Table of Contents

## Not Dead Yet

## One Out of Four...

## The Whore of Babble On

# The F-Word

# The Boys Who Run With the Dogs

I was sitting on the patio at the Black Bull drinking an Export, eh? I was staring at the wide blue sky, my mind perfectly blank, my body numbed into a Zen-like state by the burning ball of a sun which, like a laser, was searing archival images of our time into my corneas. Images like "French's Yellow Mustard", "the round red ball" and "cigarette ashes in the wind."

Words of wisdom floated to me in the hot summer breeze, brushing gently against my pineal gland like a cat rubbing against my leg — gentle, soothing, amusing slogans and acronyms, such as, "Here we are now / Entertain us" and "EMI." I shrugged off these distractions from my Total Oneness With the Sun and immersed myself completely in the true inner meaning of the sky (which, after a while, I noticed was not exactly blue but more a smoky yellow colour, tinged with pink). Every muscle in my body was completely relaxed — exhausted, really — after a long, sweaty night of wrestling with damp sheets in my living room.

Here we are now, don't entertain us. I imagined my hand, limp, trailing in the water under the moon, just like that woman in the painting *The Death of Elaine*. I was basking in the realm of the senses, watching the deep purple aureole of the sun grow larger, like the rings in a pool of water into which a stone had just been thrown.

Suddenly, a shadow rose before me and eclipsed the sun. It's a Boy! No, a Man! No, a Boy, with gleaming yellow eyes and little blond hairs that sparkled in the black light of the sun.

"Who are you?" asked the Boy, baring his teeth at me in a smile or snarl. I followed his dirty hand as it pushed his hair away from his ear, which he scratched at rapidly with one filthy, black-crescented nail.

"You want to know who I am?" I asked.

"Yes," said the Boy, as he licked his beer and planted his tongue at the corner of his mouth where it lolled like a baby in a cradle.

"I am one of the Women Who Run With the Wolves. I stalk the Intruder. I hunt. When I smell the Blood Scent, I give the Cry. I howl. I backtrack and loop. I Eat Your Sins. I am the Exposer of the Crude Shadow, the Navigator in the Dark, the Slayer of the Sacred Secrets. I make Shadows. I am the Spirit Child who can hear the Old One's Call. But oh, I am Fierce. I am the Wild Flesh from the Clan of the Scarred. I am a Woman Who Runs With the Wolves, plus I can stand on all fours. In other words, I have my little rituals."

"Yeah?" said the Boy. "Yeah, well I read that book, too." He lapped again at his beer.

Spotting a young woman wearing tight, black bicycle shorts across the patio, he whimpered a bit and then looked back at me, pleadingly, reproachfully, like a mother-in-law trying to make you feel guilty.

"May I ask who you are?" I barked.

"I am one of the Boys Who Run With the Dogs," he barked back. "I sniff the air. I roll in dirt. I tear the flesh off the bones of animals with my teeth at that Rib Place at Yonge and Eglinton. Me and my kind, we have our little rituals, too."

His yellow eyes glowed as he went on, as if he were reliving every experience as he spoke. "We like to chase the bunnies. We like to round up the sheep with their big, soft eyes and nice curly hair. We chase the cat until it's up a tree. At night, we like to bathe in the fountains." He picked up a pitcher of beer from the next table and poured it over his head. "We like to stake our territory by going for a piss. I've pissed in every bar in this city," he stated proudly. Then he snarled at the Dogs at the next table, who were still playing poker despite the loss of their beer. "They won't mess with me," he growled. "That's because the Boys Who Run With the Dogs like to travel in packs. We chew on leather. We know of rawhide. We bring the newspaper! And we like to chase the jobs!"

The Boy began to whirl around and around on the patio in a manic dance. "I chase the job around and around in circles and it makes my owner laugh. I like to have my ear scratched. I like to run in the park with the other dogs! I like to dig in the sandbox! I like to hide the rock!"

The Boy stopped singing and looked at me, one eyebrow cocked. "Say, would you mind buying me another beer? I was supposed to go meet one of the other Dogs who owes me money, but I want to stick around because there's a girl dog over there whose bum I want to bite."

I shook my head. "No." The Boy got down on his knees and stuck out his tongue. He was begging. I told him to sit. Instead, he lay down, rolled over and asked me to scratch his belly. He was an impossible, lovable dog but, being a Wolf, I found his whining and happy dancing beneath my dignity.

"Listen, Boy Who Runs With the Dogs," I said, "do you play fetch?" The Boy nodded eagerly.

"If you go to the store and fetch me cigarettes, I'll buy you a beer." The Boy leapt to his feet. "Guard my beer!" he growled as he jumped over the patio fence and ran down the street.

A while later, he trotted back from the store, the cigarette pack in his teeth. After some pulling and tugging, I managed to get the pack from him and then he curled up at my feet and fell asleep. I almost felt sorry for having lied to such an innocent young pup, but I'm sure he'd tear me to bits and bring my remains to the Prince of the Land if he found out I am really one of those Women Who Waddles With the Ducks.

# Canada Post Menstrual Syndrome

Thursday, 8:30 a.m. "Today I'm going to do something about my life," I say to myself. "I'm going to get rid of that big heap of laundry in the corner, clean out the cupboards, plant some tulip bulbs, cook up two weeks' worth of spaghetti sauce and pluck my eyebrows. Then I'll redo my résumé and go to yoga. But first, I think I'll haul that broken dishwasher out to the curb as the sight of it displeases me... In fact, maybe I'll get rid of everything in my life that displeases me! Maybe I'll get rid of that old couch, too. If it depresses you, throw it out, I say. Get rid of it! It's bad energy!"

I bound out of bed and rummage frantically for something to wear. This top makes me look pregnant! This sweater is too scratchy. These jeans have a broken zipper. No. I refuse to wear a pair of black leggings. (What am I? Some kind of reject from the eighties?) I start rustling through the closet. What did I buy this gold lamé cocktail dress for? I never wear it. This blazer needs dry-cleaning. This skirt doesn't fit. I'm getting fat. I have nothing pretty. I HAVE NOTHING PRETTY TO WEAR! I WANT TO FEEL PRETTY! I WAS NEVER PRETTY! I WAS THE UGLY ONE IN MY FAMILY!

My sisters, they all got pretty things for Christmas, didn't they? It was all jewellery and ribbon and bows for Little Miss Prim and Little Miss Perfect, while Ol' Four Eyes here got notebooks and moustache removal cream. It's the truth. I might as well admit it! I'm stupid and ugly and everybody knows it. You know why my sisters got married and I never did? It's ALL MY PARENT'S FAULT.

Why should I dress up, anyway? Why should I go to all the trouble? So that I can attract more *men*? Why do I need another man in my life? So I can lend him more money? SO HE CAN LEAVE ME AND MARRY SOMEONE ELSE AFTER FIVE YEARS OF ME SUPPORTING HIM WHILE HE LIES AROUND THE HOUSE? Hell, no! I am powerful in my life. I am not like other women. They're so catty. They watch you being clubbed over the head and dragged off by some Neanderthal, and do they feel sorry for you? No! They act all jealous instead.

It's best to have nothing. As long as you have nothing, nobody can hate you. The minute you're successful, people — especially your best friends — try to hold you back. It happens all the time. Somebody puts out a film or book or something and everybody else just stands around pretending it didn't happen. What a bunch of smugly fucklings! The world is filled with UGLY SMUGLY FUCKLINGS!

What's the point? I am not going to wear clothes today. Who's going to see me anyway? I throw my coat over some men's long underwear and set off to buy Tilex to scrub the filthy scum off my shower door. On my way to the store, I run into one of my many clients.

"Donna," she says, looking at me strangely, "did you leave the house wearing nothing but your long underwear?"

"Yeah. So? What if I did?" I snap. "And guess what — I didn't brush my hair, either! I'm an artist and I can do whatever I want. So, when are you going to pay me for all that work I did for you last September. Huh? Huh? Maybe, when your company finally gets around to paying me, I'll finally be able present myself in public like a decent person," I laugh maniacally.

"Uh, sure," she says. "I'll, uh, put that cheque in the mail right away."

Once I get to the store, I forget what I came for, so I buy a *National Enquirer* and a box of Turtles. On the way back, I see a mailbox. That bitch! She knows there's a postal strike on. I have a short, satisfying fantasy about firebombing the box. Then I have another short, satisfying fantasy about spray-painting, "Merry Christmas, Assholes! Love, Canada Post," all over it.

Back at home, the phone rings. It's my old friend Troy, in town for a short visit. "What are you doing here?" I snap. "If you think I have time to meet you, you're crazy. I have to put in the tulip bulbs today."

"Donna, there's six feet of snow on the ground," he says.

"Don't you use that reasonable tone with me!" I warn.

"Donna, do you...by any chance...have PMS?" he asks gingerly.

"No!" I scream into the phone. "I do not have PMS! Why do you men always accuse women of having PMS just because they happen to be in a bad mood?"

Of course, I'm lying. I know darn well that I have PMS. Lying about PMS when you know darn well that you have it is one of the classic symptoms.

I used to believe that PMS was just another insidious media byte fabricated by the Man to "Keep the Bitches Down." Then I quit drinking. Now I only believe that when I actually have PMS. Before, I didn't even know I was suffering from it, because my answer to any and all discomfort was to go out and drink ten glasses of red wine. Alcohol, after all, is an excellent anti-inflammatory. Now there's nothing to do but go to bed with the tabloids and a box of Turtles.

In the meantime, I'll just wait it out and hope that nobody — especially that striking mail carrier who is *deliberately* holding my hard-earned cheques hostage — gets hurt. Now, everybody just F-OFF!

# The Female Misogynist

People like to think that misogyny is an art practiced exclusively by men. I happen to believe there is such a thing as a female misogynist. Let's face it. Women screw other women over every day. This is a very unpopular subject because we "sisters" have to look like we're smiling and sticking together, even while vigorously plunging knives into each other's backs.

No, I wouldn't be a good feminist, a good witch, if I didn't portray all women as nurturers tending to each other's inner children. I'm supposed to ignore the fact that women talk behind each other's backs, sleep with each other's mates, call each other names, steal each other's jobs and resent each other's success? Pretend we don't insist that other women pay the same cruel price that we did for our emotional and social security, once we've reached the top? Yeah, right.

The women that will try and screw you over the worst are usually the ones that consider themselves to be the hippest, most socialized and most powerful. However, a girl doesn't have to be a Power-Mad Bitch to be a female misogynist — she just has to really hate women. And there are a lot of women out there who really hate other women, even more than they hate men — or themselves.

Female misogynists tend to abuse each other in covert, sneaky or devious ways, using nuance and subtlety to accomplish their wicked work. What follows is a list of symptoms to help you distinguish a potentially toxic, harmful bitch from a possible true best friend.

### The Gatekeeper:

She's usually a wordless, unsmiling executive secretary or sullen supervisor. You know she can be friendly because you've heard her being chatty and animated on the phone. Yet she treats every civil overture from you like an impending rape. Her goal in life is to keep you in the dark about everything for as long as possible. She is like the dog Cerberus at the Gates of Hell. She knows her male boss, Satan, is responsible for years of personal misery and oppression. However, she will do everything in her power to prevent you from getting in Satan's good books. Hates women because she doesn't know any other way.

## The Honest Type:

Uses the guise of honesty to consistently insult or embarrass you. This is the good friend who will scream, "Hey, you finally plucked your eyebrows!" when you're in the middle of an intimate chat with an object of desire. This not-so-subtle saboteur will also blurt out things like, "You look really fat in that dress," to undermine you, because, like a four-year-old child, she just can't stand seeing someone else get any attention. There is a more authoritarian version of the "Honest Type" who will make you feel as badly as possible about an already bad situation by acting like an advisor. She'll say something really helpful like, "To be honest, if I were you, I would kill myself." Hates women with unconditional love.

## Little Miss Misery:

Can be compared to the hand that sticks out of the grave in the horror movie Carrie and tries to pull you under with the dirt of the past. If something bad happens to you, she's right there, reliving the entire drama with you in lurid 3-D. But she's the first one to sneer if you suddenly become successful, and may even try to smear you by telling others what a sad sack you really are. Little Miss Misery loves company. Hates women because no one hurts as much as she does.

## The "I'm Addicted to a Dick" Type:

She's a fabulous person with a wonderful boyfriend. You, on the other hand, might as well be a chair, a doorknob or a vase. This kind of misogynist shows her hatred of you by forcing you to focus completely on her boyfriend at all times. She may even do this after they've broken up. Hates other women because at the moment, other women don't exist — just him.

### The Leader of the Coven:

Uses gossip to gain power over others. She gets a "high" from betraying another woman's confidence, even if it means that woman will really suffer. Will gladly phone you up and offer unsolicited information about your ex-boyfriend because she thinks you might be "interested". She might even have a little chat with him just so that she can find some purpose in life as a conduit of painful knowledge. Hates other women because they have a life.

### The Daddy-Focused Dickhead:

This kind of woman acts one way when it's just the two of you together, and another way when there is a male in the room. If there's a conversation going on, she won't meet your eyes but will filter everything through what the man says and back to you. This is her way of letting you know she knows which side her bread is buttered on. Secretly she thinks that true feminists get ahead by humouring men or behaving in stereotypical "feminine" ways. The sad fact is, nothing she does is valid without the approval of the nearest male. Hates other women because they can't provide her with security.

Women act like misogynists because they secretly believe that women are inferior. Who can blame them for this when we keep behaving like we do? Me, I'm proud of my own misogyny. I hate the women I've described above. I really do. I hate them for screwing me over, not to mention themselves and the entire women's movement, every single chance they get.

Hey, at least I'm the Honest Type.

# Watching All the Girls Go 'Bye!'

"Hey! I like your dress!"

The woman walking along Queen Street quickens her pace. Her body stiffens slightly, and she holds her head up very straight. She is an urban professional in her mid-forties, wearing a modestly cut summer dress.

"I said, HEY, I LIKE THAT DRESS!"

The woman casts a nervous glance over her shoulder in the direction of the two men sitting on the patio of The 360. One is short and fat with a bald spot crowning a glorious mane of long, dark hair. The other is tall, thin and blond and is wearing a pair of kid's sunglasses. A pitcher of beer on their table gleams in the sun like a giant amber gem.

"Hey! What's wrong with ya?"

The woman manages an insecure smile that slowly falters into a look of embarrassment. She hurries past, as if she has just remembered she has something very important to do. The two men cackle into their pints of beer. They sound like duelling Wicked Witches of the West.

"All women are stuck-up bitches. The only reason they dress that way is because they're trying to get your approval. They do it on purpose," grunts the bald one. At the next table, where my head is buried in the newspaper, I feel my left eyebrow raising like Spock's. Don't make me come over there, I think to myself.

Baldie slams his pint of beer down on the table. The flab on his thighs jiggles as he jogs his leg up and down. "They want you to say something. Then they get mad when you notice!" He is staring into the distance like the Marlboro Man, but I know his words are meant for me. "All women are stuck-up bitches!" he pronounces loudly. I look down at my chest to make sure I am still a woman and to confirm that he is, yes, actually saying this to one of these mysterious, unpredictable creatures that may just whack him on the head with a beer pitcher.

He takes another swig of his beer. He tilts the glass upwards, suckling on it like a baby goat. "I like tits!" he yells at a young woman as she rollerblades by. "Hey, I *really* like your shirt!" he bellows at a corpulent woman with huge breasts who is pushing a baby in a stroller. The breasts bounce jovially by. "Gimme some!" He roars with laughter.

The blond guy suddenly swivels around in his chair and flashes me a friendly smile.

"Don't mind my friend, eh?" he says, almost by way of apology. "It's his day off."

"Do you always wear a dress shirt with shorts?" I ask. The blond guy looks down at his outfit. He is wearing a long-sleeved rayon dress shirt with a pair of cotton shorts.

"What, you don't like what I'm wearing?"

"See?" says the bald guy, turning his raisin-brown eyeballs, the kind of eyeballs in which you can never actually see the pupils, in my direction. "All this time she's been pretending to read the paper, when actually, she's more interested in us."

"Actually, I'm more interested in reading the paper," I claim, a bit peeved that he is right. "Who can concentrate with you yelling all the time?"

"Nah, she's like all the rest." He points to a woman wearing Daisy Duke-type cut-off shorts, walking on the other side of the street. "You see her, over there? She's the most stuck-up bitch I ever met. But I still fucked her."

The blond guy bobs his head up and down. His eyes are round with awe. "He did."

Two other women who are sitting on the patio get up, grab their coffee cups and move indoors. The guys watch them move away, a slight look of disappointment on their faces.

"See, you're driving them all away," I say.

"You're not a stuck-up bitch, are you?" says the blond guy.

"Oh yes, she is," says Baldie.

I look at the blond guy. He looks at me.

"Don't get involved," he says.

There is a tense silence. I bundle up my newspapers and throw some money on the table to pay for my coffee.

"Hey!" says Baldie. "We're just watching all the girls go by. It's a lost art."

"I'm impressed."

"Oh, I'm sorry, Your Majesty, did we *disturb* you from reading your newspaper?"

"Hey!" says Blondie, by way of apology again. "I know it's a little early, but we're a little drunk."

"We're going to sit here all day, get drunk and watch the girls go by!" shouts Baldie. "It's a free country, and nobody is going to stop us."

Down the street, a young blond woman wearing white shorts bends over to lock her bicycle.

"Oh golly, wait a second — Will you look at *that*! WILL YOU GET A LOAD OF THAT ASS? Hey, I like your ass!" Baldie and Blondie start pounding on the table and hooting. The woman turns around, stares directly at them for a minute, and then comes straight for them, a severe look on her face.

"Here she comes," giggles Blondie. "She likes you."

The woman comes onto the patio. Baldie grabs one of the handles of her backpack and pulls her over to the table. The woman rolls her eyes.

"I wouldn't do that if I were you," I say.

"Why not?" pouts Baldie.

"Because I know her and she's your new waitress and she can cut you off." The waitress nods. We smile at each other.

Dejected, the two men look at the empty pitcher, now glinting like the Magic Crystal Skull in the hot noonday sun.

"You mean you're not going to bring us more beer?" whines Blondie. The waitress shrugs.

"Then we'll just go sit somewhere else and watch the girls go by!" Baldie yells after me as I leave the patio. "It's a free country! It's a lost art! You can't stop us. Please bring us another pitcher of beer…"

"Please?"

"Just one more pitcher? We'll behave." They smile like naughty four-year-olds begging for a cookie from Mom. The waitress looks back at them like a hardened defense lawyer with the weight of the world on her shoulders, even though she must only be about twenty-six.

"We'll behave."

The waitress goes inside to get their pitcher.

As I bend over to unlock my bike I hear, "Nice ass!"

# I Know You Are, But What Am I?

I am a great mystery. What am I?

I am the invention of a language that is not my own. What am I?

In my time, I have been compared to many animals. When I was young I was called a chick or a kitten. Those who thought of me fondly called me a bunny, a ducky or a filly. Those I displeased referred to me as a bitch, a pig, a cow or a nag. If I was shy they called me a mouse. If I aroused lust I was branded a minx, a beaver, a pussy and a vixen. As I aged they called me an old bat, an old bird, an old crow. What am I that is like so many animals?

My appearance has been compared to a bag, a dish and a doll. I have been named "slag", after the slag heap. I am a scrubber, a trollop, a Jezebel and a floozy. Some have described me as pinmoney. Poets have described me as porcelain and pretty. Sometimes I am referred to by an aspect of dimension. Example: broad. I am dowdy and drab, blowzy and a gab. I can be bad, rad, very, very cool or hot! No wonder so many men refer to me as "stuff", as in, "Did you check out that stuff?"

What am I that is such a riddle? Sometimes I am just "it", as in, "Are you getting it?" Sometimes I am "any", as in, "Are you getting any?" If I express my sexuality I am a slattern or a slut. If I don't I am straitlaced or frigid. I am the Ice Queen. I am Juicy Lucy. It is not unusual to have my whole being reduced to a single part of my anatomy. As in, "Hey Legs!" or "tit," as in, "Got to get me some tit." What am I that is so many things, anything and it?

I am a weapon. I am the old ball and chain, a battleaxe, a pain.

What am I that is so threatening? When I am perceived as strong I am an aegis and an amazon. Circean. A virago. When I am perceived as chaste I become a maiden. Vestal and Virgin. What am I that is so strong and chaste?

You are what you wear. I am a bluestocking, a muff and a petticoat. I am the "skirt" walking down the street. What am I that this clothing contains? I am compared to a container. A hose and a honeypot, a dish and a vase. I am a vessel. My hips are the cradle of civilization. What am I that carries this weight?

The ability to deceive is often attributed to me. I am cunning and cute. When I say no I mean yes. When I say yes I mean no. I am a cocktease and a coquette. I am an enchantress. My nicknames are Delilah and siren, Medusa and witch. I lie? What am I that is so irresistible that men fear my charms? I am a destroyer. I am banshee and crone. I am hag and harpy, Venus and vamp. I am a snatch and a scamp. A succubus. I'll suck the life right out of you. I'm a hooker. A manhunter. A nutcracker. Jaws. I am a tart, a cherry, a crumpet and a honey. I can be cheesecake. I'm a piece of meat. My genitals have been compared to seafood. What am I that is so delicious?

I am often described as a wound. I'm a crack. A gash. A rib from Adam's side. I am less than a person, known only by a part of myself. What am I that is so amputated?

I do not speak. I chatter and gossip. I am a harridan and flibbertigibbet. I am the Whore of Babble On. I have many secrets. What am I that has been denied expression? I'm a molly, a sister, a sheila and a squaw. I'm a scold, a tomboy, a biddy and a strumpet. I'm loose. I'm a silly old goose.

What am I that is so emasculating? I'm your anima, your sister, your lady, your maid. I am androgynous, butch; a feminist, a dyke. I'm the ugly duckling and the swan. I am hysteria itself. I'm frail. I am your mother. I am nymphet and nymphomaniac. I am a womb. I am a flower, the burning bush and the inside of the whale.

What am I that is so dangerous and safe? My presence is an anathema and an aphrodisiac. I am April, August, Easter, Europe, Friday, June, May. I am Cassandra. I am an invention of language, and language was invented to describe my sex. I am the C-word. What am I, then?

I am your beautiful bride, your courtesan and your concubine. I'm your missus and mistress, hussy and fishwife. I'm the fuckin' queen, the girl of your dreams. I am also your worst nightmare. What am I?

I'm the Madonna and the whore. I'm a bit, a fluff, a hole, a Jane, a nooky, a piece, a screw and a twat. I'm a babe, a lass, a moll, a suffragette, a prude, a sister, a dame, a biddy, a hussy, a slag, a snatch, a sorceress, a crack, a gash, a jamtart, a bawd, a tramp, a trollop and a tomboy! I'm a flibbertigibbet and a piece of ass, and best of all, I'm Daddy's little princess.

Do you know what I am? I am woman. Ask the Sphinx.

*Alternative names for what could simply be called a woman sourced from Woman Words: A Dictionary of Words About Woman by Jane Mills (Free Press/Maxwell MacMillan Canada).

# The Resurrection of the Cock

Like a jar of Tiger Balm left open in a room for many days, the phrase "the resurrection of the cock" has permeated my life lately. I'm not sure where I first heard this exciting rumour, but hey, if cocks are being resurrected, I want to be there.

Perhaps I first heard it from the publisher of my first book last year, when he trapped me in a corner of a certain book critic's loft to brag about his latest literary line-up. I gathered that these writers were evidence of a phallus-worshipping frenzy that will soon rape and pillage the false female idols of this culture.

I have also heard the term slide casually, in a disquieting way, from the wise old lips of artists, photographers and bookstore owners, who historically have always been two steps ahead of any uplifting renaissance in Canadian culture.

I've thought I heard my male friends whispering "the

resurrection of the cock", like Freemasons muttering the secret password, on wet street corners. I fear I will never be invited into the Lodge to watch the Grand Poobah pump his joystick, no matter how much I am compared to a female Charles Bukowski or Hunter S. Thompson. (Little do they know that I privately think of them as male Donna Lypchuks.)

The penis, from my point of view, is not to be feared or reviled. It is to be celebrated as a valuable tool that, if treated reverently, can elevate a girl to great heights. It is pointless to try and control a penis, the same way it is pointless to try and control a bad puppy. People are attracted to the idea of the resurrection of the cock because it implies a kind of release from control. After all, how can we be a bunch of free-spirited Dionysians when we're always dealing with our fear of the great battering ram or the all-consuming vaginal cave that sucks you into the void and smothers you? How can we create when we are so ruled by fear? Genitals are metaphors for cultural control: conflict and creation. So please don't hold my vagina against me.

My great deep-thinking female friends have also whispered cryptically of the resurrection of the cock. There is a poet who resurrects the cock by using an image of a rapist and serial killer to hawk her latest book — an extreme attempt to identify with the male dark side. The Mother of All Art on Queen Street sees this resurrection physically manifest as huge, glassy towers disguised as "Lofts for Sale."

An art dealer spoke of this resurrection to me two months ago — of wolves howling at the moon, serial killers and whisky bottles being featured in paintings. Filmmakers have been celebrating misogyny, as have authors, as if the fictions were hysterically funny. In fact, any cultural expression of misogyny should be taken for what it is: a parody of our deepest fear. You are what you accuse. I predict that, a few years from now, any Woman Who Runs With the Wolves will look beside her and there will be a man, happily running beside her too. And I predict that this will make them both glad.

I find the phrase "the resurrection of the cock" fascinating, as it solidifies certain vague ideas published three years ago in a Necrofile called "The Men Are Back!" This phrase came up again the other night at a party, where Scott Symons compared his participation in a documentary to being "fucked in the face by a Tyrannosaurus Rex wearing Easter bells." I like gratuitous metaphor. He also said, "Women are more dangerous than men. They know that a good hard-on is a gift from the gods."

Right. Quite frankly, an impotent male (and you don't have to take this literally) is useless to a strong female spirit. The idea that male power is something to be feared, a harbinger of violence, is getting really tired. Conversely, the idea that women have become nothing but evil male despots with an extra hole in their bodies is equally tedious. Only a very immature spirit would succumb to such fears.

But everywhere I look I see examples of this insecurity being marketed to us. I am particularly disgusted by a TV commercial for Dove soap, in which a petulant, androgynous, Gen-X guy lies on a couch and talks about how Dove is one-quarter cold cream, and how he would never read the tabloids because they are bad for his brain. This carefully thought-out ideal of the "weak" male character is anathema to me. Every time I see his smug, sensitive face, I just want to kick his butt for being such a wuss.

Furthermore, I am sick of books by men that read like they were written by a whiny thirteen-year-old girl. However, I have the wisdom to realize that this is part of the male attempt to reconcile himself with his hated feminine side.

If the cock *is* being resurrected, I still think I have yet to see real evidence of it. I guess I won't know it's happening until it fucks me over.

# Is Ally McBeal Funny?

I like watching Ally McBeal every week. I don't watch it because I think it's funny. I watch it because *horror* is my favourite genre.

Nine o' clock on a Monday night: that's the time I set aside in my life to scream and scream again at yet another terrifying, sick and twisted male projection of what a modern woman of the nineties is — you know — really like.

You can tell Ally McBeal's character was created by a man, because she exists in a state of relentless eroticization. Her wet, slippery rubbery lips, minus the usual cupid's bow, are always shown as slightly parted, as if waiting to receive a tongue (or more famous part of the male anatomy) inside her mouth. Her lips are slimy and baby pink — unpleasantly reminiscent of moist labia. The only woman on TV with a bigger euphemism on her face is Lisa Rinna from Melrose Place. (I read in a tabloid somewhere that Rinna's blown-up suckers became so obscenely obvious that Aaron Spelling ordered her to have them deflated.)

Ally is supposed to be a yuppie, but she looks like a giant, blonde guppy, breathlessly gasping "duh, duh, duh" behind the glass bubble of my TV screen. Her mouth is permanently agape, like that of a baby bird waiting to be fed. The "worm" Ally has been waiting for, however, was scooped up by her "early bird" colleague, and now Ally has to look at their happy relationship every day. This perpetual state of unrequited desire is justification for the male writer to give her that "hungry look". Ally gulps, drools, sucks on her fingers and licks her lips to innocently express her horniness. The writer didn't mean to portray Ally as seductive — these are just nervous mannerisms that reflect her spiritual starvation as a professional working woman! She just can't help the idiotic way she is…really.

I am also horrified by the show's basic premise: women can't cope because they are slaves to their biological clocks. Ally McBeal is a rationalization for the failure to fulfil potential, as in: "I'm glad I'm not more successful, because I might start hallucinating and disassociating and having panic attacks every day just like Ally!" From watching the plot so far, it is plain as day that Ally will continue to suffer symptoms of obsessive compulsive behaviour, paranoia, schizophrenia, attention deficit disorder, low self-esteem, megalomania and manic depression until she smartens up and has a baby.

Furthermore, Ally's mental problems, which are more a reflection of the writer's hatred and fear of women than any reality-based concern about having a baby before you're thirty (try forty-five, guys!), are genuinely scary. Ally is a perpetually assaulted Betty Boop, often shown drowning, choking or fighting for her life. Sometimes the writer demonizes her by giving her a long, darting tongue; this is the destructive Lilith in action. What if women really had long probing organs? They would be evil! Don't give them power! Don't let her near your cock!

The dancing baby that she dreams up is also a perverse miniaturization of some sicko's sexuality. No baby looks like that. It is not even anatomically correct. Its arms, shoulders, neck and legs have been elongated digitally so that it will look realistic as it dances. The baby itself, with it's grinding hips, secretive smile and seductive movements, has been virtually "sexualized" by a computer. Of course, McBeal herself is nothing but a giant infant — a pink rosebud waiting for a male pacifier. Even the way her head lolls lazily on her neck reminds me of a two-week-old baby whose spine is not yet developed enough to support its head. I find it hard to laugh at somebody who reminds me so much of a helpless infant, but apparently the writers are appealing to the pedophile that lurks inside the collective unconscious of America. In a disturbing way, Ally McBeal's bad posture, cowed shoulders and forced coquettish demeanor remind me of video footage I've seen of JonBenét Ramsey. Ha, ha, ha. Keep those laughs comin', boys. America loves a mentally ill woman with low self-esteem.

This show is like Roman Polanski for feminists. Ally McBeal has three basic modes. The "normal" Ally walks around with a stupid, wide-eyed, slightly surprised expression on her face, as if she has just been goosed from behind. Every time I see her with this look I think, "She wishes." I wonder how many men watch this and think the same thing. The horror film addict in me has seen that same startled look on people who have just been stabbed in the back. Sometimes she looks like she's about to start drooling, and though I want to laugh, I don't because I've been taught that one shouldn't laugh at those who appear disabled. The second is her "breathless excited mode", in which she looks flushed and consumptive, like somebody who has just finished masturbating in the bathroom crossed with a TB patient waiting for the oxygen tank to roll in. The third is her inquisitive mode, in which the actress cocks her head like a small furry animal with bright eyes who, because of a genetic lack of brain cells, can't help but be fascinated by the world. Laughing at Ally McBeal is like the stepping on the gas when you see a startled deer in the middle of the road.

One recent episode was particularly terrifying. Ally takes a female co-worker into her office and shows her how to "make love" to a caffe latte while her male co-workers spy on them. McBeal takes the foam from the coffee and, in what is the closest thing to some kind of "cum shot" that I've ever seen on TV, the camera closes in on the stuff hanging off her tongue while McBeal moans on and on in orgasmic ecstasy. I'd call it sublimated pornography, but I have too much respect for pornographers to do that. It was like watching Hans Christian Andersen's Little Match Girl getting jerked off on, right in the face. It was an act of televised comic brutality that transformed everybody's favourite crazy orphan into a child/whore. Yes, let's laugh at that debased innocent as we watch her lick the "fantasy cum" from her lips. See, she likes it and so should you. The ratings show that this is what all of America really wants — semen dripping from the child/whore archetype's labia-like lips.

Me, I'm just glad the poor anorexic-looking little thing finally got some protein.

# Forty-Eight Ways to Tell If Your Man Is a Feminist

Most men are feminists!

Yes, it's true. It's the dirty little secret of the patriarchy. Most men are basically nice guys, and if you're a man and you can

identify with most of the qualities on this list, you can rest assured
that you are a feminist. You can go around town and brag proudly
to your pals that you are a feminist. Most men love feminists. They
just don't realize it when they're going out with one.

Here are forty-eight ways to tell if your man is a feminist — even
if you're not!

1. When you're watching TV together, he lets you work the remote
every now and then.
2. When someone criticizes you for not shaving your legs, he says,
"So what? I don't shave mine either."
3. He doesn't open the door for you, but he doesn't let it slam in
your face either.
4. He always walks *with* you. He doesn't get in these moods where
you're forced to walk two or three paces behind him.
5. He thinks his mother is a goddess and would never dream of
calling either her or you a name.
6. He doesn't make fun of Michele Landsberg.
7. He does the dishes and doesn't make a big deal about it; you
know, like he just built the Taj Mahal for you or something.
8. He doesn't refer to your breasts as "hooters."
9. He doesn't refer to your gay girlfriends as "those dykes."
10. He doesn't perceive every woman who doesn't pay him enough
attention as "some kind of lesbian."
11. He buys birth control at a rate equal to yours.
12. He would never say something like "women are taking all the
jobs" because he realizes that women have one-sixth of the high-
paying jobs in this society. (We do, however, have most of the
really lousy low-paying jobs.)
13. He can say the word "feminist" in a calm, rational manner,
without raising his voice or prefacing it with a word like "fucking",
as in, "What are you, some kind of fucking feminist?"
14. He doesn't blame the fact that he doesn't have a job on "fucking
feminists" or pay equity; he realizes that the reason he doesn't have
a job is because he sat in a bar and drank himself silly for three years.

(You know this for a fact because you were sitting right by his side the whole time!)

15. He likes to watch *Mary Tyler Moore* reruns with you on WTN.

16. He brings you along to the strip club with him.

17. He doesn't think that battered women get hit because they "keep going back for more."

18. He doesn't enable his deadbeat friend to avoid paying child support by lying about his financial status to his ex-wife/girlfriend.

19. He's got a Riot Grrrls T-shirt.

20. He doesn't resent having a female boss.

21. When sexism happens to you, he doesn't smile, shake his head and say that you brought it on yourself for being feminist.

22. He thinks the hair under your arms is "very Parisian."

23. He's proud to go to the store and buy Tampax for you.

24. He will admit there is a 50/50 possibility of a chance that God could be a woman.

25. When you take him to the Women's Day march, he doesn't try to pick up other women.

26. He doesn't sabotage you or try to embarrass you in public for being successful.

27. He doesn't call an actor of the feminine persuasion an actress.

28. He's got a poster of Pamela Anderson Lee in his bedroom. That's right — Pamela Anderson Lee is a feminist icon.

29. He plays pool with you without making faces or giving you a half an hour of instruction in that condescending tone before you make a shot.

30. He doesn't expect you to pay for the entire restaurant bill because you're a feminist.

31. He doesn't refer to feminists as "man-haters."

32. He lets your male child play with dolls.

33. When you mention the word "Madonna", he doesn't cringe as if he's scared of her.

34. He doesn't let other men put you down or call you names.

35. He's fascinated by witchcraft. What man isn't?

36. When he meets your feminist friends, he doesn't automatically

assume that your "dyke" friends want to have a threesome with him because he's so attractive.

37. He doesn't tell you that it is unfeminine to be angry.

38. He reads feminist philosophy every now and then because he's interested in what's on women's minds nowadays.

39. He doesn't shriek like you're going to castrate him every time you pick up a knife to cut some vegetables.

40. When one of your girlfriends calls, he makes sure he gives you the message instead of conveniently forgetting to let you know.

41. He doesn't even know who Barbie is.

42. When your nipples get erect in a cold room, he doesn't shout, "Look everybody! Headlights!"

43. He doesn't make his secretary bring him coffee like she's some kind of love slave or something.

44. He thinks the French language is inherently sexist.

45. Every time he hears about an abused woman, he doesn't immediately snap back with a comment such as, "So what? I know plenty of men who have been abused."

46. When you tell him Pamela Anderson Lee is a feminist icon, he says, "Cool."

47. When his friends ask him, "What's with your girlfriend? Is she some kind of fucking feminist?", he nods his head proudly and says, "Yes."

48. He doesn't stutter when he has to utter the word "M-M-mother."

# In Praise of Older Women

In praise of older women (which in our society means over twenty-five):

• An older woman can wear any hat she chooses and nobody will laugh. A younger woman wearing the same hat will always look like a lampshade in a brothel.

• An older woman will never wake you up in the middle of the night to ask, "What are you thinking?" An older woman doesn't care what you think.

• An older woman always totes a purse full of emergency supplies. Younger women go hungry and bleed to death every time there's a natural disaster.

• An older woman always carries a condom in her purse. A younger woman is still hoping the guy might have one on him.

• An older woman is a cheaper date: a younger woman will cost you twelve beers, but an older woman will sleep with you after a cup of herbal tea.

• The older a woman gets, the stronger her libido gets, while the older a man gets, the weaker his libido gets...which is why nature intended young guys to go out with older women, and young women to go out with older men.

• An older woman can wear bright red lipstick during the day without looking like she just had an adventure inside a jam jar. This is not true of younger women (or drag queens).

• Older women can run faster because they're always wearing sensible shoes.

• An older woman is into free sex! An older woman is almost always attached to someone, so there's no need to develop a phobia about committing to her. The last thing she needs in her life is another clingy, whiny, dependent lover!

• Older women are more honest. An older woman will tell you that you are an asshole if you're acting like one. A young woman will say nothing, just in case it means you might break up with her. An older woman puts *herself* on a pedestal.

• If you act immature enough and hang around long enough, an older woman may mistake you for one of her children and let you live at her house rent-free. Older women can afford to support you.

• An older woman will never get pregnant and then suddenly demand that the two of you get married. In fact, if you impregnate an older woman, you will probably be the last to know.

• Older women have jobs with dental plans. Younger women can't help you when your teeth get knocked out playing hockey.

• An older woman will never accuse you of using her. She's using you.

• Older women take charge of the situation: an older woman will call *you* up and ask for a date. A younger woman will wait by the phone forever.

• Older women know how to cook. Young women know how to call for pizza.

• An older woman will introduce you to all of her girlfriends. A younger woman will avoid her girlfriends when she's with you, in case you get any ideas.

• Older women are psychic. You never have to confess to having an affair because somehow they always know.

• Older women often own an interesting collection of lingerie, acquired from admirers over the years. Young women often don't wear underpants at all, thus practically eliminating any possibility of a striptease.

• Older women know what Kegel exercises are.

• An older woman will agree to go to McDonald's with you for a meal. Younger women are too nervous to eat anything in front of somebody they might possibly boff later.

• Older women are dignified. They are beyond having a screaming match in a public park in the middle of the night.

• Older women are experienced. They understand that sometimes, after twelve beers, a boy just can't get it up. A younger woman may need some time to grasp this fact.

• An older woman has lots of girlfriends...and most of them will want to boff you, too.

• An older woman will always meet the minimum height requirement to go on an amusement ride.

• An older woman will never accuse you of stealing the best years of her youth because, chances are, someone else has stolen them first.

# My Little Monica

There's a joke that goes: "What do you call that soft, fleshy thing attached to the end of a penis?"

Answer: "A man."

Ah, yes, the first day of spring does call such breezy, wonderful insults to mind as yet another glorious mating season begins...

It is a well-known, proven and much mocked-by-women medical fact that the minds of men are ruled by a higher power: the penis. Many women have heard men describe their penises as almost possessing a kind of über-soul, or as being separate entities with a will of their own that conflicts with a man's common sense. This is why it is so difficult for a woman to trust a man. What rational adult would trust someone who believes that he is not actually responsible for his actions, and that a dangly bit of flesh between his legs makes all the decisions? What a convenient explain-everything-away kind of loophole!

To top it off, the penis is known for its moody and temperamental ways. I feel sorry for men: imagine surrendering your common sense to a manic-depressive — always up and down and up and down.

The conviction most men have that their penis is somehow separate from the rest of their body — a one-eyed, winking, weeping, little person sticking out from the groin like a miniature evil twin (quick, call David Cronenberg) — compels them to give them Christian names such as Peter, Junior and Woody.

Now it's time for me to reveal yet another special female secret in this column: women are ruled by a higher power as well — the vagina. This is a much less widely known fact. Unlike the penis — which is indiscriminate and, quite frankly, stupid — the vagina possesses the wisdom of the library of Alexandria. The vagina is a storehouse of information, just like a little old lady's purse. In fact, I found my boyfriend's missing car keys up there the other day. Just kidding.

Unlike a penis — which is shallow and can be compared to a demagnetized compass, pointing in whichever direction it feels like according to the laws of randomness and chaos — the vagina is deep, very deep. The penis, like the Cyclops, is a big, dumb, one-eyed monster. But the vagina has lips, and it talks. Yes, my vagina talks to me, whispering vile ideas late at night.

Like men, most women name their genitalia. If you are one of those shy women who have never thought to name your vagina, I strongly urge you to do so as quickly as possible. (Hurry up — it's almost the year 2000.) Unlike a penis, which never grows spiritually, a woman's vagina matures and changes with her, which is why I like to rename mine every few years. When I was younger, I used to refer to it as Brookie because it was so innocent and yearning, like Brooke Shields. Then, in the eighties, I began to call it Oprah, in homage to the famous talk-show host, because it was always bleeding and weeping. Unlike the brutal and thoughtless penis, the vagina is an empathetic entity, sensing another's need to be engulfed and sheltered. Now that I am older and have apparently reached my sexual peak, I like to refer to my vagina fondly as My Little Monica, in recognition of how its wayward and wicked ways have the power to destroy the world.

Yes, in my latter glamour years I have found that the vile whisperings of my vagina have come to exert a strange hold over me. For instance, just the other day I was having a conversation with my vagina in a café. It went something like this:

Me: That man over there looks attractive.
My Little Monica: Owww blimey, look at that one! [*drool, drool*] I'll bet he's a goer.
Me [*looking around the café wildly*]: Shut up. People can hear you.
My Little Monica: (*slobber, slobber*) Look at his ass, heh, heh, heh.
Me: Procreation is a sacred act. I'm saving myself for that special someone who will commit to me and treat me like a human being.
My Little Monica [*evilly*]: If he fucks you, it means he loves you.
Me: I don't know... [*considering for a moment*] He's attractive, but his eyes seem a little close together.
My Little Monica: Waaaah! Waaaah! But I love him. I feel so

empty without him. I love him. I want him. Now! Now!
Me [*beating about my pubic area with my hands while people stare*]:
Shut up! I mean it. Shut up!
My Little Monica: You're a cupid stunt.
Me: That does it!

A trip to the ladies' room, along with the quick insertion of a tampon (or a lady cigar, as my mom calls them), took care of that Little Monica brat. In the meantime, I've been having great difficulty explaining away the voice people keep hearing emanating from my knickers. Rather than tell people that mysteriously, over the years, my vagina has evolved in intelligence and developed the capacity of speech, I have been telling them that I am just practising my new ventriloquist act.

# Love is a Grave Mental Disease

# It's Mating Season!

Love is in the air. And everywhere you look, there are signs that another Human Mating Season is finally here.

In the morning, otherwise very proper young women strut bowlegged in their high heels on their way to the office, as if they have just spent the last eight hours riding a mechanical bull. Dehydrated-looking young men arrive late for work, chugging down bottles of Gatorade and gulping chunks of cheese in an effort to replace the precious bodily fluids and essential proteins lost the night before.

On the subway, women with faces made up like kabuki players bat wide Barbie-doll eyes at silent, sullen simian beasts who somehow during the last two weeks have shed their plaid flannel skins and miraculously developed the power of human speech.

At night, the bars and patios are full of these magical creatures. Not quite understanding exactly what's happening to them, they numb their normally excellent sense of judgment with copious amounts of a common depressant called alcohol in order to cope with their suddenly strong and violent urges to copulate with anyone who comes along.

It is a well-known fact that human beings are unable to reproduce unless they have created some sort of alternate reality for themselves. Getting drunk so you can get laid is an ancient and highly respected human mating ritual, without which many of us would not be alive today. This ritual is necessary because human beings are born with an innate hatred not only of each other, but also of bizarre gymnastics and sleeping in wet nests.

When people procreate, the actual purpose of their coupling is often the very last thing on their mind. The female of the species often mistakes this quite frankly absurd-looking physical act for a display of affection on the part of the male, and a commitment that he will spend the rest of his life with her. The male, who at this time of year often wears running shoes so he can get away from the female right afterwards, sees his co-copulating female as a kind, willing orifice who will let him practise until he can actually mate with Cindy Crawford.

The male is always surprised by the female's insistence afterwards that they are now mated for life, and he can't believe her outraged sense of abandonment when he makes it clear that he wasn't responsible for his actions at the time. The woman thinks she is feeling some sort of love, when in reality she has literally OD'd on pheromones. Love is a grave mental disease, and when you are crazy, you can rationalize anything as a choice, rather than admit to having been a pawn in Mother Nature's plan to have us re-populate the earth.

You can see these freshly mated couples on street corners everywhere, passionately hashing out a post-coital argument. Usually, the human female is quite young and cries out to the world in her dismay and confusion, while the male brusquely acts out his anger at being so cruelly tricked by human nature. Sometimes the male's subliminal instinct to care for a helpless baby of his own causes him to project those childlike qualities onto the female, who, with her large, pleading eyes, reminds him of a helpless infant. So they end up being a couple. (That is why so many men call their girlfriends "Babe".)

Like most animals, human beings never think about the results of their actions at the time of their mating, which is why they are always shocked and appalled when, a month or two later, their union produces a small sperm sculpture which often must be removed from the woman by a professional. It is ironic that we so easily accept the miracle of cloning and test-tube babies, but every time one of us spontaneously reproduces, we can't understand how it possibly could have happened. This is Spring Fever's culmination — a moment of supreme mutual stupidity that neither party can seem to admit to.

Even more mysterious to most baffled couples are the new cases of herpes, cervical warts and AIDS that pop up like spring flowers each year at this time. That's what you get for participating in a macabre parody of procreation. Mother Nature abhors a vacuum (especially the abortionist's), and if she can't grow a baby, she will grow something else in there instead. Don't rock the Cradle of Civilization unless you want to start something... big.

Human mating rituals have evolved over thousands of years into a process that is specifically designed to produce the opposite effect of what you intended when your eyes first met those come-hither looks across that smoky room — a baby, a marriage, a mortgage. Every bar should have a sign in it: If You Drink, Don't Fuck. It doesn't matter how smart you are. No one is immune to Spring Fever. So gird your loins and guard your freedom. You don't want to be busted by the laws of Nature for an FWI.*

* Fucking While Impaired

# A Matter of When...

The Bill Clinton scandal reminded me of a conversation I had with an older male friend of mine I hadn't seen for some time. He's the kind of person who asks you how you are and then puts his hand on your arm and says, "Yeah, but how are you *really?*"

Of course I began to spiel off the events of the past two years of my life, which soon began to sound like episodes of *Melrose Place* along the lines of: "...and then Billy cheated on Allison with Amanda, only Allison didn't know it, and then Amanda had an affair with Michael, and then Michael cheated on me with Taylor, etc...." I ended with: "...and now I don't speak with the whole fucked-up, immature, spiritually bereft, backstabbing lot of them!"

It's funny how truly sad and idiotic your personal life sounds in retrospect when sped up and told to someone you used to discuss your personal dramas with daily.

The conversation then turned to the number of women we knew who had been cheated on by their spouses or were currently being cheated on and didn't know it...yet. And yes, there are a lot of you out there. We talked about the beauty, strength and unconditional love that some of these women, dependent and stuck with children, had demonstrated by forgiving their husbands and going on with their lives.

I began to rehash all the times I had been cheated on and the unpleasant ways I had found out about it. There was the Great Cuckold, when all my girlfriends knew that I was being cheated on for months and let me discover it only when the new couple walked hand in hand through my door. Any objection automatically made me the Enemy of Love — no matter how long I had lived with or supported the guy prior to this emotionally devastating event.

Then there was the time my roommate took a fancy to a part-time fuck I was involved with and brazenly took off with him the night after I had had sex with him. I am particularly impatient with women who don't even wait for my saliva to dry before they make their move. In fact, I recently lost a female friend who kept trying to justify her bad behaviour — necking with somebody's boyfriend while the girlfriend stood over them, screaming for them to stop — by describing the injured party as being "obviously crazy." Traumatized maybe, but not crazy.

Another time, after having asked my live-in boyfriend if he was having an affair with Ms. So & So (which of course he denied), I came home from work early and walked in on them rutting like crazed weasels. If I'd had a weapon in my hand, two people would now be dead.

After making my friend relive this stuff, I immediately started berating myself for all the bad choices I had made. My lousy judgment. My lousy taste in men. My lousy taste in girlfriends who behave like stunned beasts, following the most popular Judas Cow and thinking nothing of kicking other girls when they're down.

Every day I mourn the fact that I seem to attract nothing but untrustworthy emotional gougers, for whom truth is merely a matter of convenience. Every day I beat myself up thinking that I must be responsible for these situations — after all, nobody treats you like a doormat unless you have "Welcome" written on your forehead. Right?

Wrong. "You're not going to like it when I say this, Donna," said my friend, gently. "But the next time you go out with a guy, remember that it's not a question of *if*, as in, 'I wonder if he'll cheat on me,' but rather a question of *when*. If you would accept this one truth about male nature and treat cheating as an inevitability instead of something to be reviled, then you'd have no reason to beat yourself up."

This was the first time I had ever heard these words uttered by a male. Women always talk about it, but hearing a man admit it was really quite something. Apparently all men are cheating dogs. I don't have any evidence from my own life to support any other claim, but I maintain that women are the biggest enablers of this behaviour. If women are capable of making choices and, because of their mercurial nature, men are not, then it's obvious who is responsible for all the cheating going on. I am only comforted by the fact that I know some of these self-styled sirens — those women that men cheat with — live in a paranoid hell in which they must constantly monitor the actions of their stolen trophy; in which every phone call, every letter, every social event is a potential threat that may offer their hard-won male an opportunity to cheat again.

After all, even the transformative powers of your special love can never change another's essential nature. For these women, like their female victims, it's only a question of when.

# The Way to a Man's Heart

They say the way to a man's heart is through his stomach. When I first heard this, I was about twenty-two and took things literally. I was hovering over my boyfriend's abdomen with a scalpel when it dawned on me: "Oh — they mean *food*." So I put down the knife and made lasagna instead. But the lasagna had spinach in it, and my boyfriend didn't like spinach, so he left me. (At least I *think* it was the spinach.) That was when I first learned to respect the awesome power of food.

Let's face it, women have been using food to control others for centuries. The most obvious example is Eve, offering Adam a bite of forbidden fruit. Ever since then, women have been hovering over cauldrons, trying to stir up magic potions. You see, men live in Paradise as long as they are single. The apparent goal of the modern-day Eve is to get man kicked out of Paradise so that he can live in Co-Dependent Hell on Earth with her.

There are many ways this can be done. The first brutal, directly carnal method is to serve the man food that actually resembles female genitalia, such as figs or raw oysters. Hopefully, the man will associate what's on the plate with what you have under your skirt, making it occur to him to ravage you. Another way is to draw the guy a diagram — serve two eggs sunny side up like two breasts staring at him, or a dessert topped with a mammarian mound of whipped cream and a cherry. The idea is to lure the man into your lair by creating pleasant associations: serving him cakes that look like wedding dresses, stuffed birds with spread legs, the thighs dripping with butter — any pornography on a plate that may cause him to make a pleasurable connection between the food and you. If you really want to get subtle and sophisticated, you can resort to aromatherapy. Apparently the scents of vanilla, cinnamon and, ahem, apples cause the man to lose his senses and jump you, which is why it is always a good idea for the modern-day Eve to keep an apple pie bubbling away in the oven.

After a couple of years of marriage, the purpose of cooking switches from seduction to causing permanent disability. Last week I saw a very interesting program on the Food Network. I didn't catch the title, but it may as well have been called "How to Hold Your Man Hostage With Food." In this program, four fifty-plus crones from Edmonton hovered over a dish called (I kid you not) Weekend Spouse Saver. They were fussing over this dish with the steely, sober concentration of coroners conducting an autopsy. Huge wedding rings shone on their white knuckles, which looked like they would suckerpunch any bimbo who dared give their husbands a sidelong glance. They wore the uniform of their coven: a greying fringe of bangs (for that youthful Dorothy Hamill look), pastel sweaters over plaid shirts and pearlescent foundation that gives aging skin that unearthly glow.

These women meant business — they had survived the potential apocalypse of their 25th wedding anniversaries and were there to advise other women how to become a member of that elite. Their eyes glittered as one woman held a knife aloft, like a high priestess about to commit a ritual sacrifice, and then chopped in a manner that seemed to be a metaphor for the castration of some Randy Andy's organ. This was more than just cooking; it was magic.

The Weekend Spouse Saver was a recipe for impotence, a perversion of basic lasagna. Making it was not unlike making the marital bed. First a layer of sodium-laden yellow corn chips was laid on the bottom of the pan. This was covered by a layer of artery-clogging ground pork and Monterey Jack cheese, and then a layer of tiny, green, gastritis-friendly jalapeno peppers. Soon it became apparent that these women were involved in some kind of murder plot in which their men were fated to die in their arms, *and not anybody else's*, at whatever cost — even if it meant killing him with this food. The idea seemed to be to disable the spouse so that he would be too busy farting, belching and coagulating fat in his arteries to contemplate having a thing on the side with the office temp or the waitress at the local bar. And even if he did, there was a plot waiting for him in the garden, behind the tulips and day lilies, and the wife would be able to live out her days as a rich dowager, smiling with her special secret.

After all, as every wise woman knows, the way to a man's heart attack is through his stomach, too.

# International No-Man's Day

Gender politics is ultimately about language, and you know what language leads to — rhetoric, semantics and all-'round confusion. No wonder men and women can't get along. I have always believed that you can tell more about a situation by what is *not* being said than by what is, which is why I find it so revealing that:

## You'll Never Hear a Man Say...

Why isn't there an International Men's Day? I love her, but she won't commit to me. She's an ambler, a gambler and a midnight rambler. We have an "open" relationship. She's a bad girl, but I love her because she's bad. I'm saving myself for her. She's the wind beneath my wings. Do these jeans make my thighs look fat? She looks really rugged and handsome with a beard. Sometimes I just like to have a good cry, and then I feel better. She only hit me that one time and she promised me it will never happen again. Why doesn't she ever phone? I get so embarrassed when construction workers whistle at me. I go wherever she goes and I'm happy. I have to do something about these laugh-lines around my eyes. Shopping cheers me up. Oh, no! I have cellulite! I got my bikini line waxed the other day…ooh, ouch! She has big feet, so that means she must have a big sex organ. I carry my whole life around in my purse. I have to pamper my sensitive skin. I think we should meet and have a nice, long talk about our relationship and the direction it's headed. I just found a suspicious-looking lump in my breast. You treat me like a sex object! I don't brag at how well I do at my job in case it threatens her self-esteem. Some days I look in the mirror and hate myself. As a man, I have special dietary requirements that are different from a woman's. I fake orgasms all the time so she won't feel bad. Women are women — they think with their dinks. I have nothing to wear. She has a fear of intimacy. I want to be with her forever. I feel used. I have needs. You're just like all the rest. Is that all there is? I never came.

## And You'll Never Hear a Woman Say...

I'm impotent. Cor blimey, look at the balls on that one! I used to love him, but I had to kill him. I'm a loner and a rebel. Hey, I did you a favour by leaving him. Nice legs, shame about the face. There goes a mercy fuck if I ever saw one. Wham, bam, thank you, sir! If only he didn't spoil everything by opening his mouth. Why does he keep phoning me all the time? If he wants to see me he knows where to find me. There are those couple of days a month when I know enough to just stay away! He led me on. He's such a cunt-tease. There goes a piece of ass! He's a screamer. He's a moaner. He's easy. He could use a pluck job on his eyebrows. Stay away from him — he's an ovary-breaker! Nice tits. He wants it...you can tell. What are you, a fucking feminist? He's good-looking so he's probably a bastard. If you really loved me, you'd let me take off the condom. Let's live together first, see how it works out and then get married. Sex is sex. Power is an aphrodisiac — men will be attracted to you no matter what you look like if you have power. He didn't mean anything to me, I swear. It's you I love — I just did it for the sex. Don't take the way I am personally — it's just the way I am. I never hit him when I get angry, I just punch a wall instead. I love you, but I'm not in love with you. You're too needy. I'm no good for you, babe. Go find someone worthy of you. I didn't want to upset you more than you already were, so I thought it best to just stay away. Forever is a long time. I wear the same socks every day. It was just a fuck — what's the big deal? Women have all the power. Every day is International Women's Day.

## Another Sordid Affair

I was really devastated when my last boyfriend and I broke up. I went through the Five Stages of Grief:
1. Walking Around Totally Stunned All Day.
2. Doing Him Favours So He'll Be Really Nice to Me Again One Day.
3. Talking My Head Off About Him Until My Friends Tell Me to Shut Up.
4. Denial.
5. Wanting to Blow His Head Off With a Twelve-Gauge Shotgun.
6. Going to His House, Sitting on His Doorstep and Crying Until He Comes Out and Tells Me to Leave.
7. Phoning His Answering Machine and Hanging Up Without

Leaving a Message.
8. Cutting Off All My Hair and Smearing Cigarette Ashes On My Forehead.

Until finally, the last stage of the process…

9. Acceptance.

Wait a sec, that's more than five stages. But I feel much, much better. I now have the power to recognize an abusive man when I am attracted to him. You know, the alarm bells just go off. Some days the inside of my head sounds like the beginning of that Pink Floyd song "Time".

I have danced the Dance of Anger, mostly in nightclubs with strangers to songs like The B-52s' "Love Shack", and healed the child within by hanging a Native American dream catcher in my window. I have recognized that I attracted these bad relationships because I WANTED to be abused. It was ALL MY FAULT. I now know that it was a good thing my last boyfriend left me homeless and broke, to rot and die alone. By leaving me, he was *actually* doing me a favour. People ask me now why I put up with it. I nod solemnly and tell them simply, "It was My Path."

I now realize that I am a People Pleaser who has lived her life, thus far, for everybody else, but that the only time it is appropriate to behave in that selfless, namby-pamby, co-dependent, people-pleasing way is if you are being paid $8 an hour for it as a greeter at the Gap. I have learned my lesson about men, and I swear that I am never going to fall for a jerk again. I swear it on my copy of *Creating Co-Dependency*.

Enough about the ex-boyfriend. I am in a new relationship. Let me tell you about my new beau, Satan. *Yes*, Satan. Don't judge a book by its cover.

From the moment I met Satan, I had that feeling — you know the one — like I'd known him for thousands, maybe millions of years. It was like he knew my every secret thought and desire. And he didn't remind me of anyone I had ever met before, which my therapist tells me is a good thing because the minute you are attracted to someone who reminds you of somebody from your past — such as weird Uncle Archie, your first boyfriend or your high school guidance counsellor — that is your clue that you are doomed to repeat your pattern of shame and abuse. No, Satan was unlike any other man I had ever met. For example, Satan never seems to be without cash. He's into real estate and shoes — something to do with soles.

When I first started going out with Satan, who sometimes uses the pseudonym Ned Dickens (not be confused with the local writer and theatre director of the same name), my close friends objected because they thought he was a bit "flashy". I usually go for that moody, romantic, disappointed idealist type — you know, the one with the leather jacket, the bike and the part-time job, who spends all his time drinking so he can make contacts to get his *real* career as a poet or artist or whatever off the ground. Quite frankly, it's refreshing to be with someone who isn't overwhelmed by their own personal insecurities. You'd never catch Satan at a party staring sullenly into his beer while willing you to leave because he resents the fact that you have other interests besides him. You'd never catch Satan flirting with other girls, coming home drunk or whining about not being able to make the rent. No, he's too busy making deals.

Aside from being charming, confident and well-dressed, Satan is not afraid to express his feelings for me. He's always sending me little notes and gifts, and he's not into me for cab fare or extra beers like all the rest. All he says he wants in exchange is my eternal soul. Isn't that sweet?

I don't mean to imply that our relationship doesn't have its problems. For instance, after we had been going out for a few months, Satan started making like we weren't going out at all. I sat down and had a talk with him, explained that we had reached the three-month crisis point in our relationship and that we needed to commit to each other. At first he was kind of evasive, but then he agreed that if things were going well in a few months, we would move in together on a trial basis.

I keep telling Satan how much I love him, and he's so sweet, he even says things to me like, "Hey babe, you should get another guy. I'm no good." But I've made up my mind. I know he can be kind of evil, but he's humble, has a wicked sense of humour, is a snazzy dresser and really knows how to throw a BBQ. I feel as if Satan is part of my personal breakthrough. So far he's turning out to be the best boyfriend I ever had. With a guy like Satan for a beau, how could a girl go wrong — again?

# I Hate Valentine's Day

Valentine's Day is that day when you are expected to do something "special" for the *one* you love. The emotional communist in me starts thinking, "Nobody in your life should be *that* special."

Why does love have to have a class structure, with romantic love as the ideal at the top and other kinds of love below it? Shouldn't we be loving everyone equally? Why don't we have a day that celebrates true love in its purer, less selfish, less physical forms — a day to celebrate benevolence and compassion? Whatever happened to the concept of loving the one you're with? Isn't it nobler to love everybody all the time as best you can than to hoard your love for that one "special" person? Particularly when half the time that special person doesn't love you as much as you love them, or vice versa? I maintain that love that has to prove itself isn't love at all; it's an ego trip that has more to do with inflating the person doing the giving than with loving the object of desire.

Valentine's Day reeks of desperation, uncertainty, anticipation and despair. I think they should rename it Co-Dependent Hell Day. Valentine's Day celebrates conditional love: "I only love you as long as I can stick my penis in your vagina. That's the deal. In return, you get this box of chocolates and a bouquet of roses." What the hell is that? That is almost as twisted and sick as the concept of marriage: "I will marry you as long as I get to stick my penis in your vagina. That's the deal. In return, you get this ring and a piece of paper."

True love isn't about making deals like a couple of lawyers under the covers. True love is antithetical to the very concept of Valentine's Day, which is all about having unrealistic expectations of a "special someone". Often these expectations are thought of by one or both partners as needs. They aren't really needs at all (who needs a negligee if you are truly turned on?), but rather delusions that need to be fed to a monstrous emotional artifice that the couple dreamt up together. This Frankenstein, also known as the "we of us", must constantly be patched up, restuffed and fed with fantasies lest it rear its ugly head to gobble up both partners and send them into the nothingness of an ego-void. Philosophers would say that being ejected into the nothingness of the ego-void is actually good for you, an opportunity for the veils to be stripped from your eyes so that you can be led onto the path of true love. The cornerstone of these philosophies is that you cannot love another unless you love yourself first, which is why it might be a good idea to send a Valentine to yourself on Valentine's Day.

The last thing most of us want is to hear any truth about the human condition; we prefer to project qualities of an ideal onto a person, as if they were a movie screen. You see this all the time — the battered woman who projects childlike innocence onto her abuser, or the older man who projects intelligence and talent onto a younger woman because she meets his ideal of beauty. Then we throw tantrums or get depressed or obsessed when the object of desire doesn't follow the script we set up for them. This state of mental illness is what our society calls love. Valentine's Day reinforces the idea that love is blind, that we should have unrealistic or idealistic expectations of those we love and refuse to see them for who they actually are. It is the favourite holiday of the terminally bitter, disappointed idealist, which is how most people describe themselves after some kind of romantic movie of theirs gets chewed up by reality.

In our society, many grave mental disturbances are defined by the saying, "It must be love." If you have a desire to control someone, it must be love. If you have the desire to change someone "for their own good", it must be love. If you have the desire to stay with a person at any cost, it must be love. If you are obsessed, it must be love. If you lust, it must be love. These are all symptoms of something, but it is not love. I don't believe there is any truth to the term "crazy in love". If you feel crazy, you probably just are crazy, and not in love at all. If you are "lovesick", you are probably just plain sick, and not in love at all. Love doesn't have symptoms. Love is nothing special, unless there is something wrong.

# Lies Women Tell Men

## Part I: The Courtship Phase

No, you're not boring! I like to hear you talk. It's...interesting. Marriage is stupid. You would be a lot further in your career if it weren't for all those bastards holding you back. I believe that nice guys finish last, and you're a nice guy, so that's why you are where you are today. I never want to have children — there are too many souls on the planet already. Yes, you do look a lot like Val Kilmer, especially with that haircut! When I'm with you I feel like a real woman, instead of just a girl. I feel safe when I'm with you, unlike any other man I'm around. Hold me, I'm scared. You're the first man I've ever met that I could truly call a feminist. You're smart in a way that most men aren't. I'm terrified of intimacy and have never found a man who could get through to me. Oh, I had a lesbian experience...just once, though. I don't mind picking up the tab. I don't mind paying for the cab. I'm not interested in your body, I'm interested in your mind! My other lovers would just die if they knew I was with you right now. I don't think I could have sex with you because sometimes it hurts to put my tampon in.

## Part II: The Consummation

Oops, I must be really drunk. I'm sorry — I don't know why, but my hand just sort of went there. You look sexy in those boxer shorts/long underwear/torn underwear. I love to feel a man's beard on my chin. Yes, I took my birth control pill last night. I love to swallow. Hmm, quite the handful. Oooh, ow, I think you're too big for me. Yes, I came. No, you're not hogging the bed, I have plenty of room. The sound of your snoring at night is comforting. It's OK if you just throw that used condom anywhere. Nobody I ever slept with has AIDS. I'll never forget how wonderful last night was. No, I understand perfectly why you would want to keep this relationship a big secret and not announce it proudly to the world!

## Part III: The Beginning of the End

It would be cheaper if the two of us lived together. So what if you'll be sixty-five when I'm thirty? Age doesn't matter if you love each other. I don't talk to my girlfriends about you — that would be wrong! Your mom's really nice. No, you don't have a receding hairline; you just have a high forehead. You would make an excellent father. I know that you would never lie to me. You'd really get along with my parents. I respect the fact that sometimes you need your space, and that when you ignore me, it's nothing personal. I'd rather spend my time with you than go out. I don't need your approval. I love the way you're so honest with me. I know you love me, you just have trouble expressing it. Oh, I know you would have phoned if you weren't so busy. Oh, I kiss everybody — that's just the way I am. Not tonight, dear, I have a headache.

## Part IV: The End

It's not you, it's me. I'm to blame for everything that is wrong in our relationship. Oh, he's just a friend. My feelings for you are so intense, I can't handle being with you any more. I really value our friendship, and I don't want to destroy it by having sex with you. I'm going to be very busy for the next few months. I was too drunk to know what I was doing the first time I slept with you, so I'm really sorry. My best friend is infatuated with you, so if we keep seeing each other, I'll lose her as a friend. You're so attractive that I just can't compete with all the other girls who are attracted to you. I'm confused about my sexuality, and I need some time to think it over before I sleep with any man again. My astrologer says our signs are incompatible, so I don't think we should continue this futile situation. I've had such a twisted childhood that I'm not capable of having a relationship with anyone, ever. No, I'm not jealous of your new girlfriend. Thank you for letting me stay overnight and not making it sexual. I hope you and your new girlfriend will be very happy. I never lie.

# Toying With Affections

I received an exciting new press release the other day, and I thought I would be the first writer in town to share its novel contents with you. There is absolutely no need to waste one more valuable minute of your life performing some antiquated mating ritual to attract a member of the opposite sex. That's right: valuable Canadian dollars, formerly spent on excess hair removal, cosmetics, just the right jeans, cab rides to nightclubs and six or seven lip-loosening, thigh-opening beers can now be safely invested in a mutual fund or RRSP. Thanks to a new invention, the Virtual Lover, you can put yourself through all the emotional convolutions, screaming, fighting, power struggles, suicide threats, illnesses and repeated lessons in relationship existentialism, without having to spend more than $19.99. Never, ever find yourself having to cover his share of the rent! Never, ever be left sleeping in the wet spot!

According to the press release, from Retail Results Corporation, this new invention is "the most exciting new electronic game since Virtual Pets, geared to a wide age range of primarily female buyers from seven to fifty years old." Obviously, the marketing geniuses behind this toy have figured out that only women have the time to spend cultivating and nurturing a fictional relationship with a small stick figure created by liquid crystal display. This saves them from wasting their time cultivating and nurturing fictional relationships with real-life men. Somehow those marketing people know that a man may be tempted to indulge in a 9 1/2 *Weeks* scenario with the stick figure, initially pleasuring it and then leaving it to suffer alone in the top drawer of a desk.

The Virtual Lover teaches you to how to manipulate and control others emotionally like you never have before. In order to "meet" your new lover, you must input personal details for both of you, including your birth dates, blood types and genders. All of these details will affect your compatibility. Different choices create different relationship needs. There are 480 different relationship combinations — more men than a girl could meet in a week of scarfing down martinis at the Bovine Sex Club. This is definitely a game for those who believe in the principles of determinism. Fate does not play a role; co-dependency does. You choose your torturer.

According to the press release, "the game requires you to take care of, entertain, communicate with and buy gifts for the electronic boyfriend or girlfriend." Any first-year psychology major will tell you that these conditions have already set your new virtual relationship on the road to disaster. It is obvious that the Virtual Lover, so dependent on you, will always have the upper hand. You could easily end up in a nurse/patient relationship, such as one might find with a real-life alcoholic or drug addict. The idea that you must somehow entertain your lover constantly brings up sordid images of women desperately wrapping themselves in Saran Wrap to distract their husbands from the TV. The concept that you must endlessly buy it gifts teaches us that you must bribe others to gain their affections. If I had a Virtual Lover such as this, I would find myself screaming, "Hey, little liquid crystal display stick man, what about *my* needs? What do you do for *me*?" Then it would die or leave me for a rival, and I would feel guilty and have to spend years with a psychotherapist.

The game also encourages you to become a control freak. The press release tells us, "You must arrange your electronic character's activities, which include working to acquire money [many of us have been left in real life for merely trying to introduce this novel concept], studying and maintaining your appearance to please your friend. If you do not pay enough attention to your friend, they may die or leave you."

The game obviously does not take into account the Virtual Lover's sense of free will. You, the budding seven-to-fifty-year-old dominatrix, tell him when to sleep, study and work. He, in return, will base his decision of whether to leave you on your personal appearance. Hey, I guess the inventors of this game are just telling it like it is! Although he is programmed to sleep through the night, he will only study or work for two hours at a time. Like any mentally-ill character, this means that your possessive Virtual Lover will be bothering you with his numerous crises, his little beeps and buzzes, just like a real-life pager, preventing you from working or paying attention to anyone else. Oh sure, you can shut off the sound on the thing, but like that real life lover whom you once hung up on after he threatened suicide, you will constantly be worried about whether he is going to go through with it. Interestingly enough, the press release describes this game as a tool that "teaches good life management skills — especially for teenagers."

Described as a "relationship training aid," the Virtual Lover does have one feature that impressionable young minds will hopefully not take literally. In this game, unsatisfactory relationships can be ended with the click of the reset button. In real life, unsatisfactory relationships can't be ended this way unless, of course, the click in question comes from the barrel of a gun.

# Steal Pay
# for This Book

# Originality Is My Trademark

As a writer, I pride myself on the originality of my material. The fact that I am able to do this week after week is enough to Boggle™ my mind. I know most of you think it must be a Snap™, but quite frankly, coming up with an idea that does not belong to somebody else takes a lot of TIME™. Like most writers, I am deeply dedicated to my Kraft™.

Usually I sit down at my Macintosh™, and after a flick of my Bic™ and a couple of Vantages™, I am off to the races. That Second Cup™ of coffee is like Prozac™ for writers. Other times, however, I wake up in the morning and feel like my brain is swathed in folds of Gore-Tex™. I feel about as sharp as a bowl full of Jell-O™. This is bad news, because originality is Paramount™ to my success as a writer.

Unlike a typical journalist, my columns are not always inspired by whatever's in the *Weekly World News*™. The mainstream media has a Monopoly™ on those stories. I want to write something that will appeal to Generation Next.™ When I'm in a bad mood, I sometimes write what I really think and that gets me in Trouble™. Occasionally, I wish I was living in the days of Lucy Maud Montgomery, when the most original thing a woman writer was expected to come up with was Anne of Green Gables™.

Sometimes the muse beckons when I'm not writing but involved in some Trivial Pursuit™, such as eating an Apple™, slurping a Popsicle™ or playing Nintendo™. Sometimes my best ideas come when I'm working on the Stairmaster™ or out on my Rollerblades™. When I get stuck, I like to put on my Ray-Bans™ and take a long walk with Fido™, especially when it's Fairweather™ and the world is a Sunny Delight™. It Pampers™ my soul. Other times I put on my Nike™s and take a nice Sprint™ around the block, except of course when there is a blizzard and a White-Out ™. A writer has to exercise or risk developing a belly like Winnie the Pooh™. I like walking, because it is the No More Tears™ workout.

When I'm really stuck, I distract myself by giving the carpet a good Hoover™ing. When I was Hoover™ing this morning, it occurred to me to take a Polaroid™ of artist Adrienne Trent at the opening of her exhibition of color Xerox™es. Then I thought maybe I could write a column about how a Comet™ is going hit the Earth, or about how the plastic in Barbie™ is non-biodegradable, or about what a Mickey Mouse™ operation the Oscars™ are. Then it dawned on me that those ideas weren't very original. Oh well, my mind needs time to Shake 'N Bake™ a while before something I can claim as my own slides out of the Easy Bake Oven™.

Some writers get their best ideas from sitting around in charming little diners with ancient Formica™ countertops Spackle™d with glitter, and getting in touch with the common *People*™. Personally, I don't like to sit in a restaurant unless I'm actually Eaton™ something. I've been thinking, now that the weather's warm, I should get out the Hibachi™ and throw a party, but I'm a lousy Hostess™. Nothing much is spicing up my life lately, except for Tabasco™ sauce. The best thing to do is lock myself in my room and live like a Quaker™ until my writing is done.

Sometimes a writer can sit in front of the computer for an Eternity™ and still come up with Zero™. Sometimes it just seems impossible to Wisk™ up an idea like Martha Stewart™. This kind of frustration can go on for days, until you just want to take an Arm & Hammer™ and smash the computer screen. A writer without a good idea is terminally on the rag — in need of some serious Tampax™ for their bleeding brain. At times like this I pop a few Tylenol™ and listen to some music on my Walkman™. Music Windex™es the windows of my mind so I can think clearly. It's like Valium™.

Like most writers, I like to procrastinate by doing something that has nothing to do with writing, like cleaning my keyboard with a Q-tip™. I am always spilling something sticky, like Coke™ or Nestea™, on my computer, so I keep a box of Kleenex™ nearby. Sometimes I even have to use a Swiss Army™ knife to get the gunk out. Really, sometimes I can be such a Dirt Devil™! All this procrastination is part of the daily Roto-rooting™ of the subconscious I do to come up with my best ideas. When I finally get an idea, I yell, "Yahoo!™"

Mostly, though, when I'm supposed to be writing I find myself daydreaming, picturing myself as a CoverGirl™ in Paris, modelling Chanel™ or riding on the back of a Harley Davidson™ with some guy. I like to imagine myself riding the Crest™ of a Wave™ on a Boogie Board™. If I imagine hard enough, I can actually feel the Ocean Spray™ on my face and the slap of the Breaking Wave™. Then, when the day is over, I'll towel myself off until I am Soft 'N' Dri™ and sit on the dock of The Bay™ watching the Tide™ come in...

# The Canadian Remainder-Bin Network

VOICE OVER: Coming up next! At 4:30 a.m.! It's the Canadian Remainder-Bin Network with your host — Carol Goodwill!
MUSIC OVER: *Theme from* Rocky.
[CUT TO: *interior TV studio. 4:30 a.m. Somewhere in Canada. Carol Goodwill, an attractive, dun-haired woman in her mid-forties, wearing a pink Marci Lipman sweat shirt, 50 per cent polyester/50 per cent cotton pink sweatpants, imitation pearls and orthopedic running shoes, sits in a comfortable-looking wingback chair against a set made completely of cardboard.*

*Sitting next to her on the couch is Canada's answer to Vanna White — Elaine (no last name), a voluptuous, beige-haired woman, also in her forties, wearing a clingy, see-through yellow Lycra top over a black bra, white sweatpants, white high heels and a crooked smile that just begs you to "name that drug!"*

*In the background, there is a dying rubber plant in a brown plastic Tupperware tub.*]

CAROL: Hi there! My name is Carol Goodwill, and welcome to the Canadian version of the Remainder-Bin Network! Today we have a number of very special items for you, made all the more special because we are Canadian, which means you don't have to pay a US surtax on any of the items you see here today like you do on the American Remainder-Bin Network! No, sirree! You pay nothing but the GST and PST! Now, let's get started!

[IMAGE INSERT: *Plastic, fluorescent-coloured comb sitting on a shiny rayon pillow slowly rotates on a carousel so the television audience can see it from every angle. Words flash on and off the screen:* COMB. Retail price $2.95. CRBN price just 14 cents. Items left: 170,000. Seconds left: 20.]

CAROL: Our first item is…a comb! Now how many times have you ladies out there looked in the mirror, noticed that your hair, you know, could use a bit of fixing and then thought to yourself, "What I wouldn't do just to have a comb right now"? Has that ever happened to you, Elaine?

[CUT TO: *Elaine smiling and nodding.*]

CAROL: Well, after some careful shopping — and remember, folks, every item that you see here on the CRBN is totally unique and cannot be acquired anywhere else — [*Phone rings.*] Oh, it looks like we have a caller. [*Carol picks up phone.*] Hello caller, go ahead!
CALLER: Yeah, I bought your comb. I bought it on Yonge St. for 10 cents. [*Carol hangs up.*]
[*Words flash on and off screen:* COMB. Retail price $3.95. CRBN price just 10 cents. Items left: 170,000. Seconds left: 10.]
CAROL: Now, ladies, I want you to note that this is not just *any* comb, as our model Elaine here is demonstrating…

[CUT TO *Elaine combing her hair and smiling brightly at the camera.*]

CAROL: This is a brightly coloured plastic comb! Ladies, I'm sure you've all had that experience as I have, where you're getting ready to go out on that big date or to that fancy dinner engagement, and you're in the bathroom and for some darn reason, you just can't seem to find that comb! Has that ever happened to you, Elaine?

[CUT TO *Elaine smiling and combing her hair. A bit of drool crawls out of the corner of her mouth.*]

CAROL: This is a comb that really stands out! Most combs seem to just blend in with the other objects in the bathroom — you know, with the shampoo and mascara and what have you, but not this comb! As you can see, this comb is brightly coloured, and you know, if you're near-sighted or have a very deep, dark purse, as I do, a comb like this can really save you time because you're not always rummaging around for it when you should be doing other things, like taking your kids to the park or polishing the silver or whatever. It's very, very handy. I just couldn't resist this incredible deal, so I bought three or four of them myself. Elaine, how many did you buy?

[CUT TO *Elaine snoring on couch.*]

[CUT QUICKLY TO *Comb turning on carousel, again.*]

CAROL: Just look at that beautiful comb! And it comes in one colour. Fluorescent Green. Now remember, ladies, we only have 170,000 of these left and only five seconds in our program for you to take advantage of this incredible offer. Look at this comb! Think of what an incredible gift it would make for someone you know! Think of all the other incredible things you could comb with it! The dog, the carpet...you could even use it to comb your wigs! [*Words flash on and off screen:* COMB. Suggested Retail Price $6.95. CRBN price just 5 cents. Items left: 170,000. Seconds Left: 0. A buzzer sounds.]

[CUT TO *Elaine waking up with a start and beginning to draw the comb through her hair.*]

CAROL: Oops! There goes the buzzer and we're out of time. For those of you who missed this unique opportunity to buy this fabulous comb, we will be selling it again at 5 a.m., 6 a.m. and 7 a.m. all weekend. Now stay tuned, we have some other incredible bargains coming right up on the Canadian Remainder-Bin Network!

MUSIC OVER: *Theme from* Rocky *up*.
IMAGE: *Paper coin wrappers turning slowly on a carousel*. FLAG: Only one-cent and 5-cent sizes left! 4:15 a.m!
IMAGE: *Key chains made to look like plastic baby pacifiers turning on carousel*. FLAG: Only 700,000 left! 4:30 a.m!
IMAGE: *Elaine's feet wearing a pair of courtesy slippers made from cotton with the British Airways logo on the side*. FLAG: Unlimited Quantities! 4:45 a.m!
IMAGE: *Elaine tugging at comb stuck in her hair*. FLAG: 5 a.m!
IMAGE: *Dying rubber plant turning on a carousel*. FLAG: $19.95. Only one left! ACT NOW!

# Read My Lips

The other day I went to Club Monaco and asked for "the Monica Lewinsky lipstick". Happy to oblige, the cosmetician picked carefully among the shiny metal shafts on the counter until she found "Glaze", the now-famous sheer tint that made Monica Lewinsky look like she'd just finished necking with a raspberry popsicle when she was interviewed by Barbara Walters.

Fascinated, I watched as the cosmetician spiralled the glistening wax phallus until it was fully erect. Just as I expected, the lipstick was a shiny, swollen purple colour; the colour of rotten plums and rotten politicians.

"I don't know why, " I gasped. "I just have to have it."

"You're not alone," said the cosmetician.

If it hadn't looked good on me, I would've bought it anyway.

They don't call me Donna Lipstick for nothing; my medicine

cabinet is full of useless tubes (penis substitutes, my sister calls them) that I bought just because the name was sheer (no pun intended) poetry, a classic, or somehow historically significant. For instance, I bought Revlon's Cherries in The Snow because I liked the image. Both Natalka Husar, the famous Canadian painter, and I bought Revlon's Love That Red because it was the same orange shade of red that you only find little old ladies in Saskatoon wearing; a kind of heritage thing. Sometimes I just buy the lipstick because I like the packaging; my most recent art purchase was a slim silver tube of Tony and Tina's Connect because the thing looks like a miniature 1950s atomic missile. (It also smelled really nice.)

Ever since I was a little girl, I have enjoyed reading lipstick tubes just for the bad puns. There's Avon's Berry Berry Nice, L'Oréal's Looking Grape! and Jane's Mauve For All and One For All.

Mostly, though, lipstick relates to food, in keeping with the line: "you're a real dish." Just about every lipstick line has a Berry, a Cranberry and a Cherry, as well as a Cocoa and a Brown Sugar. Revlon seems to be the company most into such "woman as mouth-watering meal" symbolism, with names like Very Very Cherry, Whipped Cream, Raspberry Crunch, Strawberry Sorbet, Rich Raisin Frost and Orange Flip. Then there's Clinique's Apple Butter, Sugar Bean and Black Honey, as well as Rimmell's Sugar Plum and Pink Soda. Or, for a hearty meal, why not offer your lips up to your man while they are bathed in a smooth, buttery coating of Warm Salmon by Three Custom Colour Specialists?

The dessert menu includes: Estée Lauder's Mocha Torte, Benfits's Walnut Creme and Lancie's Creme Caramel. Yes, we could kill a man with metaphorical hypoglycemia when our lips are done up in Guerlain's Orange Satin Sorbet, Hard Candy's Chocolate Kiss or Mary Kay's Cherries Jubilee.

The idea that lipstick can also make your man "drunk with desire" is not lost on cosmetic companies, who liberally name their lipsticks Champagne, Wine and Burgundy. Seduce that special alcoholic with Clinique's Golden Brandy, Plum Brandy, Grape Cognac and Claret. L'Oréal serves up Sangria and Divine Wine for last call, and Poppy offers a Mai Tai and a Piña Colada. Other shades gauranteed to get your man as addicted to you as he is to the bottle are MAC's Dubonnet, Mavala's Madeira and Milani's Bordeaux (for the more sophisticated types). Hey, Club Monaco, where's that pale, frosty Canadian shade called "Beer"?

Wearing your lipstick can also denote your social class; Black Radiance's Uptown Red directly contrasts with Hard Candy's Trailer Trash. There are also plenty of lipsticks named after celebrities — Agnes B's Marilyn Red, Benefits's Dietrich, Stila's Piaf — which, alas, won't bestow you with those women's talent. The film festival continues with Francois Nars's Roman Holiday, which will have you gleaming like Audrey Hepburn, while Manic Panic's Pussy Galore will have you grinning at your intended like a porn star.

For those of us looking to define our feminine identities according to the animal kingdom, there are a range of options. Some shades, such as Hard Candy's Pussy Cat, imply helpless innocence, while other shades, such as Urban Decay's Alley Cat, Rat and Roach, imply something less dependent. Estée Lauder's Fawn Fatale, in particular, invokes a menacing image of a wicked Bambi.

Equally disturbing are what I would call the evil lipsticks. First of all, there are those named after evil flowers: Clinique's Black Violet and Manic Panic's Deadly Night Shade and Black Lily. And every cosmetic line seems to have a lipstick called Fetish. In the general, all-'round bad behaviour category are Manic Panic's Black Witch, Kiss of Death, Damnation and White Stiletto; Hard Candy's Narcotic and Goldigger; Shiseido's Peach Lies; Trucco's Fatal and Wicked. Read my lips — what kind of girl wears a lipstick called Snob, Venus, Vixen (Smashbox), Tramp (Manic Panic), Diva or Siren (MAC)?

Some lipsticks relay direct messages to men, such as Mattess's Approachable, Revlon's Prissy, Trucco's Coy and Benefits's Reckless and Just Looking. What am I telling the world by wearing Chanel's Clandestine or Hard Candy's Tease, L'Oréal's Ready or Not, Francois Nars's Fire Down Below or Urban Decay's Headbanger? Some names even daringly allude to a state of undress, such as Benefit's Buck Naked and Revlon's In The Buff, and Urban Decay's Gash gets right to the point. Even more amazing is the number of lipsticks that refer to physical injury or illness, such as Laura Mercier's Just Bitten, Elizabeth Arden's Breathless and Urban Decay's Bruise, Asphyxia, and Frostbite. Jane even makes a lipstick that implies an allergy: Shy of Shrimp.

Then there are those names that not only have nothing to do with the colour but seem to be attempting some kind of vague social commentary. What colour is T.G.I.F. (Ultima II) supposed to be? How will I look in Myth, Skew, Ionic or Grid (MAC), Cardboard, Cash, Grafitti, Smog or Spare Change (Urban Decay)? Define the colour of Irony (Club Monaco). Yes, there is something empowering about putting on a lipstick called Goddess (Trucco) or Toast of the Town (CoverGirl) every morning, but what if you just want to buy a lipstick that's red?

Well, you've got Francois Nars's Jungle Red, Revlon's Fatal Red, Elve Von Freudenberg's Screaming Bloody Red, Lancie's Drop Dead Red, Shiseido's No Question Red and Wet 'n' Wild's Real Red — not to be confused with Alexander de Markoff 's Really Red. If you're in search of the truth about red, there's also Shiseido's Reddish, Elizabeth Arden's Pure Red, Rimmel's Truly Red and — going for the record — No. 7's Red Red, Clinique's Red Red Red and Jane's Reddest.

Thank God both Maybelline and Bobbie Brown still make a lipstick simply called Red.

## Girls Just Want to Have Fun

It's summer again, and I have no idea what I'm supposed to be doing. I mean, I know I'm a woman and I know I'm supposed to be having fun, but it's like I've forgotten what society expects of me.

So I went to the bookstore and picked out a few important cultural guides, such as *Mademoiselle*, *Self* and *Allure*, and I flipped through the pages looking for inspiration. I thought that if I stared at pictures of other women having fun, maybe I could figure out how I could put myself in a similar situation, one that might possibly lead to having fun or at least make it seem like I was having fun.

I started out by leafing through the July issue of *Allure* magazine. Immediately, I saw that in order to have fun, I was supposed to be sitting on the hood of a car parked in the middle of the desert, laughing and talking to a good friend. Oh, yes. And I was supposed to be smoking a Virginia Slims cigarette. OK. So just what are these two women doing, sitting on the hood of their car, laughing maniacally, in the middle of the desert? Are they runaways like Thelma and Louise? Are they waiting for a tow truck? Did they just pull over and decide to have a smoke? Was it too windy to light up in the car? Aren't their asses being fried sitting on that hot metal? I hope they remembered to wear sunscreen. Just what do these people think is fun? One thing almost goes without saying: the fun doesn't start until everybody has lit up.

The next thing that caught my eye was an ad for Camel cigarettes. A woman dressed in a sexy French maid costume ashes her cigarette into a pan of food she is cooking for two spoiled rich people. They obviously deserve it because they are sneering at her behind her back. Yes, it can be fun to wreak petty revenge on the bourgeois pigs, but how does one get oneself in a situation like this? (Note to self: Buy a French maid outfit. And more cigarettes.)

A flip through the fashion spreads in *Allure* suggests a couple of more interesting ways for a girl to have fun. One spread shows a woman standing in the middle of the road, apparently waiting to get run over. In some of the pictures she is alone; in others she is with her dog, family and friends. You know, this looks like so much fun that I think I'll stand in the middle of the road with a stupid look on my face right now!

Another spread shows a woman dressed in a white Donna Karan ballgown, hanging from a tree branch like an ape. This of course, never occurred to me, so no wonder I never have any fun. (Note to self: Shave underarms before trying this from low-hanging maple tree branch in Trinity-Bellwoods Park.)

The same woman is shown later, slogging through woods in a medieval chain mail and leather get-up by Versace that looks like it weighs a thousand pounds. Apparently, pretending to be a medieval pilgrim in the Crusades can also be a lot of fun. (Note to self: Get out burlap sack and walk down centre of Spadina Avenue.)

The inside front cover of the July issue of *Mademoiselle* folds out to reveal a series of pictures of a Kate Moss type having sex on top of a motorcycle on a wet street. She is not smiling; in fact, she looks like she's going to cry. Oh, my. What kind of drugs did she do to get herself in this fix? Oh right, when you're a woman, being "taken" is supposed to be fun.

Another ad, for Giorgio Armani perfume, shows a woman who has caked her face with sand. Yes, it is fun to just lie there, let go of all those un-fun adult things you have learned in the past thirty years and smear your face with sand like a two-year-old.

An ad for CoverGirl shows Naomi Campbell and some other girls making a fun part-time job for themselves by setting up a stand on the beach to sell seashells to passersby. Wait a minute. It looks like fun, but it doesn't exactly make sound business sense. Why would you buy seashells from these enthusiastic, pretty girls when you could pick them up for free on the beach? I guess they're in it for the fun, not the money.

Just as I was about to ask myself the question "Am I having fun yet?" I ran across a picture of a girl reading a fashion magazine. "Hey, that's me!" I exclaimed, and then I noticed that the girl in the picture wasn't smiling either. Probably all worn out from trying to figure out from these weird pictures just how a girl is supposed to have fun, without, you know, getting lung cancer or getting run over.

## Men Stink!

I was walking through the cosmetics department at Eaton's the other day, when suddenly, a smartly dressed woman blinded me with some vile gas.

"My eyes! My beautiful eyes!" I screamed. "What is that stuff?"

"Contradiction for Men," she said. "By Calvin Klein," she added brightly.

"Goddamn you, Calvin Klein!" I thought as I reeled through the cosmetics aisle, tears streaming down my face. I stumbled and fell, banged my head on the Estée Lauder counter and...

Minutes later, I was awoken by a man speaking in a sensitive, halting manner. You know, the way they speak when they want to let you know that they've really put some thought into what they are about to say.

"I don't want someone to need me, but I do want someone to really want me."

"What the hell is that supposed to mean?" I thought. I opened my eyes. Before me was a TV monitor displaying a Matt Dillon look-alike, leather jacket draped over his shoulder, eyes ablaze with that "You can fuck me, but you'll never understand me" intensity, and smirking mysteriously like a big old sphinx.

"I don't want someone to need me, but I do want someone to really want me," he said again. "Contradiction," hissed a chorus of women orgasmically. "By Calvin Klein."

"Fuck," I thought to myself. "If he was my boyfriend, I would punch him right in his stupid, pretty, thoughtless face." Am I supposed to fall in love with this guy because he contradicts himself? I hate men who contradict themselves. Say what you mean, pal. You know, as the drag queen, punk singer Wayne County sings, "If you don't want to fuck me, baby, baby, fuck off!"

I seemed to be trapped in some kind of fairy land, full of row upon row of bright, shiny bottles, but it wasn't the liquor store. On either side of me were banks of monitors, stacked Orwellian-style, upon which women writhed and moaned orgasmically while worshipping images of intense young men, who seemed to be fucking them and leaving them. It took me a few minutes to figure out where I was. Oh yeah, the Ministry of Aroma in the men's cologne department at Eaton's. In a pheromone-induced trance, I wandered through the aisles, picking up bottles and examining labels. Each bottle seemed to contain the essence of some obnoxious male quality.

There was Evasion, a slippery green fluid in a hard-to-get-a-grip-on bottle. "The truth shall set you free," sobbed a nearly naked woman writhing on a floor full of billowing curtains. She sat up suddenly and looked at the camera, her thumb in her mouth. A man's face was superimposed on hers. "What is truth?" he asked as his handsome visage faded away. Evasion — for the man who wants to make a woman wonder.

Next to that was Insensitive, a cool blue liquid in a tall, frosted shaft of glass. "He never calls, he never stays...He never even asked me my name," said a woman wearing so much mascara she seemed to have two black eyes. "That's because," stated a chorus of male voices, "he's so...Insensitive." A guy wearing a leather jacket smiled at the camera and roared off on his motorcycle. Insensitive — not just a cologne, but a way of being.

Other labels assaulted my eyes. Conquest for Men — a stone-shaped bottle with a bejewelled stopper that looked just like King Arthur's sword. Collusion — for the man who knows what he wants and knows how to get it...his way. Womanizer — for the man who just keeps going and going and going and going. Caligula — the cologne that turns women into beasts.

My eyes finally rested on a plain white bottle. "Sanitarium," breathed a voice on the promotional video beside it. "It can make a woman insane." On the screen a woman in a straitjacket orgasmed as a guy threw his leather jacket over his shoulder, winked at the camera and walked away. "You can't drive me crazy, I can walk from where I am."

"OK, that's it," I thought.

"Don't you have anything that isn't misogyny in a bottle?" I screamed at the clerk.

"We do," he said, "but you may not like it. We have Campbell's." He opened a stopper on a bottle and shoved it under my nose. "Mmmm, mmm, good."

I shrivelled up my nose. "What are you wearing?"

"I personally prefer to wear Star Trek for Men. Of course, Star

Trek for Men is only sold over the Internet. Type in this website address and make it so."

"Sounds like it's for nerds," I thought. "I don't want to go out with a nerd." On my way out I was gassed one more time by a dose of Contradiction. When I came to, I thought, "It's true. Men really do stink."

# Women Stink, Too!

I didn't want to go back to Eaton's after what happened last time, but I had to! It's winter, and I badly needed to buy a pair of black tights. They have the best selection of black tights at Eaton's.

So it was with great trepidation that I set foot in that famous Canadian department store for the second time in one week. Like a soldier on the beaches of Dieppe, I had to keep focused on my mission: get in, get the tights and get the hell out. Got to the cash register, paid, watched the lady put them in a bag and headed for the exit. It was easy. I could smell victory, when...

Suddenly, I was ambushed from behind by a smartly dressed woman brandishing a perfume atomizer the size of an Uzi. The vile gas stung my eyes. I steadied myself, coughing, trying not to stumble and fall.

"Oh my God, you bitch! What was that?" I screamed.

"Obsession," said the woman. "By Calvin Klein."

"It figures," I thought, clawing at my burning flesh and cursing the name Calvin Klein to hell for the second time. Succumbing to vertigo, I fell and hit my head on the Shiseido counter. When I came to I found myself suffering from a bad case of déjà vu. I was in the Ministry of Aroma in Eaton's again, only this time my disorientation had led me to the female section, where before me glittered an array of sparkling bottles featuring the latest concepts in women's perfume.

"Obsession!" hissed one of the TV monitors. Kate Moss was groaning and moaning in a state of hyper-eroticization, while a man's voice whispered intensely again, "Obsession." "Aha, methinks me spots another trend in toiletry products," I thought as I looked at the labels on the bottles around me. "And something about these marketing concepts and what they say about women definitely smells."

Lined up were similar products, all making dubious statements about the essence of the female spirit. First was the mother of all mental illness in a bottle, Obsession — the perfume for female stalkers. And Poison — for women who equate mating with destruction. Then there was Delusion. "If you believe he loves you...he will," read the placard beside it. Vulnerability ("Show him you're strong enough to be weak"). "Devastation," hissed a chorus of whispery voices on a TV monitor that pictured a beautiful woman in a diaphanous gown, slitting her wrists and falling to the floor while a good-looking guy in a leather jacket winked at me. "For the love that lasts beyond death."

There was also Lolita ("To bring out the Pretty Baby in you"), Purrfume ("For the sex kitten in you"), Deadly ("Show him you mean business"), Night Rider ("You're in control...in the saddle all night long"), Snag ("To catch that special someone"), Virgin ("For that fresh, clean, born-again feeling"), Giving ("For the nurturing woman"), Sacrifice ("Show him you'd give or do anything for him...even die"), Phallus ("For the woman who knows what matters to her")...the limbic system reels. Hey, Calvin Klein, phone me — I've got plenty more good ideas where those came from.

"My God!" I screamed. "Aren't there any perfumes here that actually empower women?"

"Well," said an older, bespectacled female clerk behind the perfume bar, "we do have Promotion. A little spray of this and hopefully, one day, you'll get promoted. We also have Brute, for those special women who feel they must impersonate a man, as well as ITILY, an acronym for I Thought I Loved You. We have Survivor, the empowering perfume for those who know the truth of what it's like to be a woman today. Can you hang on a second, dearie? I have to kick out that guy who's masturbating in front of the Obsession video." She sighed and rolled her eyes. "I guess they get us mixed up with that porn theatre up the street. Happens all the time."

While the clerk reasoned with the guy fixated on the desperate visage of Kate Moss writhing with unrequited love, I headed for the exit. On my way, I was ambushed again, this time by another woman armed with a bottle of Obsession. As I lay on the cool floor, recovering from my latest attack of the vapours, I couldn't help but think, "Men may stink, but women stink just as much sometimes."

# Victoria's Secret Is Out

It's that time of the year again. I must drop whatever I'm doing, unplug the phone and take part in a sacred rite that marks the changing of the seasons. In ancient times, people knew it was time to burn the sacrificial body of the Harvest Lord and bring in the crops when the mailman slid the fall Victoria's Secret catalogue through the slot.

The Victoria's Secret catalogue is a sacred, magical object that compels all who see it to curl up on the couch and worship its contents. Who could help but revere this random gift from the universe, which somehow wended its way to you, Occupant? No wonder it has the power to render normally conversational adults speechless.

A good hostess knows never to leave a Victoria's Secret catalogue on the coffee table because guests will be caught in its spell, ignoring all pleas for sociability with a preoccupied grunt. I once left a Victoria's Secret catalogue in my washroom, and one of my guests disappeared in there for close to an hour. We began to wonder if she was sick, and she was — sick with lust for low-waisted London jeans in every colour! After some coaxing and pounding on the door, she finally emerged, blushing and muttering, "Victoria's Secret." She didn't have to say anything more.

Unlike the J. Crew catalogue, Victoria's Secret holds a special fascination for men. In fact, if you want to meet a man, a good way to go about it would be to sit demurely in a bar or laundromat reading this catalogue. By doing so, you send out the message that you will never pass judgment on him for eating at McDonald's or for passing gas while watching the hockey game. He, in turn, will project the archetypal qualities of the Victoria's Secret model onto you. You are proud of your breasts, and you will allow him to be proud of them too. You will never shriek at him about child support or talk bitterly of the tyranny of the male patriarchy. Like many of the placid-faced models, your major ambition in life will be to stand there in your sexy underwear, waiting for him to take you when it is convenient for him. This fantasy is so appealing to men that even if they are upright, moral citizens, they will resort to stealing your copy of the catalogue to take home with them…for later. The unwritten law is that men are not allowed to subscribe. The catalogue is for aspiring satin-clad goddesses only.

Men may steal the Victoria's Secret catalogue for the pictures, but I like to read it for the articles. "Fall arrives with a cool breeze of cotton gauze," coos the copy about a super-frilly, powder blue nightgown that looks great on the model waiting for her suitor on the edge of her bed, but on me would look more like I'd somehow become entangled in the dust-ruffle on my grandmother's bed. "Nothing's quite as exquisite as the sublime feel of satin against your bare skin," the fictional Victoria rhapsodizes about a pair of men's pajamas that you could only wear once before permanently staining them with coffee. "Simple. Sexy. Perfect," they write of a floor-length, lime green cotton gown that you know would emerge from the dryer studded with those horrible fluffy nubbins. The trouble with Victoria's Secret clothing, as any woman who has owned it knows, is that all of it, even the street wear, turns into pajama wear sooner than later.

Still, even though I know it is terribly impractical to be a Victoria's Secret girl, I have always longed to be one. I would love to parade around in "a refined jacket with dress in crisp, bright white cotton piqué," but I'm afraid someone might ask me where I parked the ice cream truck. I dream of cavorting in a sleek halter-top romper in hot pink or in a sexy scoop-neck top and denim short-shorts with little strings hanging from the crotch, but I'm afraid I wouldn't be able to handle the cars that would follow me.

The Victoria's Secret girls live in a storybook world where a woman can dress however she wants and not be accused of anything but excellent self-esteem; a world where underwear never turns a distressing shade of grey and your panties always match your bra. Maybe one day I'll own a Second Skin satin bra and coordinating panties in every shade — white, ivory, peony pink, pale pink, peach, beige, gold, lilac, powder blue, silver, pale aqua, floral print and black — instead of always wearing those plaid things I got at the Bi-way with the black sports bra my mother got on sale at Eaton's.

Hey, a girl's allowed to dream, isn't she?

# Bogus Loft Living

Is it a real loft? Or is it just another small, stuffy, Toronto bachelor apartment, complete with no closet space, cardboard walls, screaming neighbours and the smells of garbage and cabbage wafting down the hallways? If you were just moving downtown from suburbia, how would you know whether you were plunking down $200,000, or so, for a real loft or a fake loft? You wouldn't. Because, unlike me, most of you have never lived in a real artist's loft, and if you knew what real loft living was like — trust me on this — you wouldn't want it.

As a bitter former loft-dwelling artist who can no longer afford Toronto's miraculous re-zoned so-called live/work spaces, I am always amused by the way these new cardboard slums are being marketed as funky studios. It is now officially impossible for a pedestrian to manoeuvre past any major street corner without staggering into a sidewalk sandwich board, sometimes even three or four of them, that screams such outrageous statements as, "Live in a Real Loft Like a Real Person!" or "Authentic Loft Living" or "Live Where a Real Artist Was Living Just Moments Before You Started Reading This!" Very often, these signs have arrows that point directly to some building in which either I or one of my friends used to live, before we were forced to rent single-floor residential units in an adjacent neighbourhood. Trust me — authentic loft living doesn't exist any more. There is only inauthentic loft living.

As a journalist who has only the best interests of the consumer in mind, I have delved deep into my Memories of Queen Street to put together this list of perks commonly advertised in loft brochures. I have contrasted them with the features that you should really look for when purchasing a genuine, authentic artist's loft from days of yore:

| Fake Loft of Today | Real Artist's Loft of Yore |
|---|---|
| Enjoy cooking on a real gas stove! | Smells like gas from automotive repair shop below! |
| Central air conditioning! | Broken window panes provide cooling comfort year round! |
| Exposed brick! | Expansive view of brick wall of building next door through only window! |
| Steps to shops and restaurants! | Scary freight elevator ride to shops and restaurants! |
| Ensuite Jacuzzi! | Blow up child's wading pool, then fill with pails of water hauled from |

common bathroom down hall. When finished bathing, yell "Look out below!" and dump contents of pool out window!

Climbing wall!

Risk life by climbing rickety ladder to futon in 12-foot-high loft every night!

Gym and exercise facilities!

Get plenty of exercise by moving your bed around so building inspector won't find out you live there!

Art gallery on ground floor!

Exploitative garment-industry sweatshop on ground floor!

Party room!

That would be the studio next door where that jerk holds nightly speakeasies!

Landscaped roof terraces!

Roof with wrecked plastic lawn chair!

24-hour concierge!

Skinheads sleeping on front steps prevent unauthorized admittance at all times!

# Joan of Art

# Free Grant Proposals!

Impress the Chalmers family with your revisionist French Film Theory! Wow Mr. and Mrs. McMichael with your Jackson Pollock-style sculpture! Yes, I said sculpture and I meant sculpture — just imagine how creative and imaginative and free a 3-D Jackson Pollock would be!

Here are some *free* ideas for grant proposals that you can use to convince this province's disillusioned cultural patrons that talent *still exists* in Ontario, and furthermore, that their millions of dollars are being put to *good use*, and that Jack Bush is not rolling over in his grave because you spent all of your grant money on a "How to Cruise the Internet" seminar instead of on a portage with easel through Algonquin Park, as promised in the application.

As an artist, whether ye be writer, painter, filmmaker or bingo dabber, it is up to you to allay the fears of rich people so they don't run away from you with their millions of dollars. So here are some awesomely excellent proposals for projects that they would be fools — do you hear me? *absolute fools* — not to fund!

## Project: The Bingo Dabber Painting Series

Description: A series of abstract paintings created using different-coloured bingo dabbers
Amount Requested: $14,000
Artist Statement: In the tradition of Olitski and other polka dot-making artists, it is my intention to expose the unfairness of the class struggle in general by using an unconventional artist's tool to display my confusion and anger at the lower classes' inherent inability to keep up with the status quo as defined by the imperialistic Western patriarchy.

## Project: The Remember Our Days of Glory Art Show

Description: Remember that really good art show me and my friends put on in 1981? Well, we would like to ask for some money to put on the exact same show again to remind everybody that we're all still around, even though in the meantime we've broken up as a collective and haven't really done anything in the last fifteen years. Well, maybe we won't put on the exact same show. Maybe we'll leave out some of the people we don't like any more.

Amount Requested: $26,000

Curatorial Statement: It is important to look back at the artists who have created art history in Canada so we can decide right now, before we die, who was the most influential artist among us. It is also important for us to take credit for all the work we did on the show before the people we have selectively eliminated from our history write a book or something.

## Project: The Birth of Rock 'n' Roll Wall Mural

Description: A Mural! Depicting! The Birth! Of Rock 'n' Roll! From Hendrix to Joplin to Devo! To Be Painted on a Wall! Somewhere! Downtown! Yeah! All Right!

Amount Requested: $3,000

Artist Statement: My my, hey hey, rock 'n' roll is here to stay is all I have to say. Oh, yeah and I promise I will spend the money on paint and not on the car or joints or beer or anything.

## Project: The Egyptian Garden in Mississauga

Description: Working in tandem with a real Egyptian, it is our intention as landscape artists to transform a landfill site in Mississauga into an Egyptian garden, complete with a red-coloured Nile River that really overflows and real papyrus!

Amount Requested: $200,000

Artist Statement: By mixing indigenous Canadian plants (such as trilliums and the tulips that Queen Juliana brought over during the war) with real papyrus, and contrasting Egyptian landforms (such as sand) with parts of the Canadian Shield (which we will transport to Mississauga from the Gatineau Hills), the public will be able to see an interesting spatial relationship between Egyptian landforms and Canadian landforms with one glance.

Project: "The Cartoons of the NFB: Figures
of a Fascist Regime or Merely Amusing?"
Description: A 3,500-word essay, perhaps to be published at great
expense to the author (photocopying, postage), in a provincial
collection of essays, to be published at any time in the next seven years.
Amount Requested: $1,500
Artist Statement: A thoughtful analysis of such NFB classics as *The
Cat Came Back* has led me to the conclusion that these cartoons are
more like reality than reality itself — the very nature of reality, of
course, being more fascist than liberal in that it keeps coming to
kick you with its big black boots, relentlessly, very much like the
cat in *The Cat Came Back*.

Project: *The Making of a Canadian Sage:* A Novel
Description: A novel about a son who lives in the shadow of his
famous father, who travels a lot between Montreal and Quebec
debating political issues while having many affairs with gorgeous
women, yet at the same time keeping a special place in his heart for
his wife, who forgives him for putting her in a mental institution
because she knows his quest to find himself as a famous Canadian
writer is more important.
Amount Requested: $10,000
Artist Statement: Please see enclosed soft feature about my eccentric
and wonderful life that was published in the *Kingston Whig-Standard*.

Project: *I'm Sick and Tired and I'm Not Going
to Take It Any More:* A Film
Description: A 16-mm, colour educational half-hour film featuring
interviews with Canada's most famous arts patrons — the
Chalmers, the McMichaels and the Tanenbaums — where they tell
you, the artist, what they think is a good art proposal.
Amount Requested: $30,000
Artist Statement: *See* title above.

# Theatre People Are Special!

Theatre People are not like other people. Theatre People are special. For one thing, Theatre People pronounce "theatre" not as "theeter", like ordinary Canadians, but as "thee-uh-tuh", as in: "I'm in the [blow smoke in your face from cigarette elegantly poised between middle and third fingers] *thee-uh-tuh*. What is it that *you* do, again?" Thee-uh-tuh people also pronounce the word "film" as "fill-um", as in: "You haven't seen *Trainspotting*! Oh, you must! It's such a fabulous fill-um!"

Theatre People also have their own special language. You know you are talking to a Theatre Person if they preface each reference to your life with the phrase "that little", as in: "How is that little boyfriend of yours anyway?" or "How's that little screenplay you're writing coming along?" However, if they are referring to their own life, they will preface their comments with the adjective "fabulous", as in: "You must come over some day and see my fabulous lava lamp" or "I have a fabulous new part in a fabulous new play."

Theatre People have the curious habit of referring to themselves in the third person. For instance, if a waiter happens to spill a drink on a Theatre Person at the beer tent for the local theatre festival, they will not react immediately, but make some comment like, "You-know-who is not pleased." If you ask a Theatre Person what they did last night they will say, "She," and you will look around to see who the Theatre Person means before realizing it is the Theatre Person herself, "was a bad girl. She went out last night and drank Jägermeister with the boys, even though she knew she would be late for her rehearsal the next day."

Although it may seem that Theatre People are quite chatty and friendly, a true connoisseur of Theatre People soon realizes that most of them have absolutely nothing to say at all. Yet they are often perceived as being brilliant conversationalists, because most of them are excellent mimics. An extremely talented Theatre Person can parrot the very same interesting anecdote that was told to you by someone else the night before, word for word, as if that experience belonged to him or her. In fact, it is not unusual for a Theatre Person to repeat back to you the exact same story that you once told them, as if it happened to the Theatre Person, because, despite their talent for memorization, Theatre People also have very short memories unless you are somehow in a position to cast them in a play.

Theatre People also fill potentially embarrassing lapses in conversation, which could reveal their ignorance about the topic at hand, by answering a question with a question. For instance, if you say, "I really liked Daniel McIvor in *House*. Did you see it?" they will respond with "Oh, Daniel McIvor. Isn't Daniel McIvor fabulous?"

Theatre People are also very fond of something they call "Drama". Usually Theatre People have studied the secrets of how to do Drama at institutions such as York, Ryerson, the National Theatre School or Trent. Most Theatre People cannot get jobs as actors in Toronto, they can only get jobs as participants in something very much like a play, called a "workshop". This forces most of them to practise their Drama in Every Day Life. Of course, the first thing that every Theatre Person learns after they take out a student loan to study Drama a University is that "the First Rule of Drama Is Conflict." Without conflict, there can be no drama. Realizing this, these nubile, aspiring thespians practise their drama by making life around them as disruptive and dysfunctional as possible. One Theatre Person will often call up another Theatre Person and say, "I'm having a crisis," so that the two of them have an excuse to get together, drink coffee, smoke cigarettes and practice facial expressions together.

Theatre People also have a gift for exaggeration. For instance, a Theatre Person never just "goes to the bathroom." A true Theatre Person "goes to perform their ablutions" or "anoint their loins". Theatre People never find themselves merely "rehearsing for a role." They are instead "summoning up the demons from their past and transforming them into angels, so that we can all be purified by the performance experience".

Theatre People are good at giving ultimatums. "If you don't come over here right now, I will kill myself" is a favourite and oft-heard line. That and, "If something doesn't happen in my career soon, I swear I'll slit my wrists." These attempts to be dramatic, which in any other country would be saved for the stage, also include screaming loudly for no reason (what Theatre People refer to as "projecting"), contorting their bodies into weird positions (what students of Drama remember as "warming up") and panting loudly in public (otherwise known as "breathing exercises").

Theatre People will tell you that they're on Prozac when they're not. Theatre People are also fond of saying, "I will do anything to get to the top, including having sex with a director or producer, if that's what it takes," when all it might take is some singing lessons.

Yes, Theatre People are special. Without them, my "little life" would be so much less…fabulous for me.

# Lady Di: The Musical

What do you think Andrew Lloyd Webber is doing right this minute? Do you think he's thinking, "A musical about the life of Eva Péron is one thing, but Lady Diana — now *that* would be going too far."

I think not.

A musical about the life of Lady Diana will be coming to a Princess of Wales Theatre near you real soon — let's say in 2002, after the initial distaste for such ventures has died down (as it were). Also in the works has to be the inevitable unintentionally hilarious made-for-TV movie starring (maybe) Tori Spelling as Diana, James Brolin as Charles, Joan Rivers as Camilla and Roseanne Barr as the evil Queen Elizabeth.

Those of you who would never lower yourself to watch such "trash" will be relieved to know that you will likely be able to watch a tastefully done feature film, starring Cameron Diaz as the ill-fated princess, Hugh Grant as her ex-hubby, Sharon Stone as his mistress, and Kathy Bates as the evil Queen. Watch for cameo appearances by Julia Roberts as Fergie and Antonio Banderas as Dodi. There's probably even a sitcom in the works — starring someone like Jenna Elfman or Téa Leoni — called *That Darn Princess*, about a wacky and free-spirited commoner who causes chaos when she suddenly finds herself thrown into the midst of a straightlaced, repressive, royal family that lives in a castle where nothing seems to work. In fact, the first hilarious episode could be about how, as the princess moves in, she blows electrical circuits in the castle by plugging in the blowdryer and curling iron simultaneously, leading the Queen to believe, for a few super-funny moments, that England is being blitzed by the Germans — again.

For those of you who think that too much attention has been already paid to the life and times of Princess Diana, just wait until the professional myth-makers get their hands on her life story. I, for one, think it's hypocritical to wait and have decided to beat Lloyd Webber to the punch. As I am not exactly a composer, I have revised the lyrics to popular songs to evoke the atmosphere of each musical number.

## Lady Di: The Musical

ACT I: THE MEETING

*The show opens with the OVERTURE and a musical number by the CHORUS, who are played, of course, by a group of PAPARAZZI, replete with flashbulb cameras. To the tune of "Pop Goes the Weasel", they do a furtive dance and then clear the stage to reveal DIANA, wearing rubber boots and a see-through skirt, standing in a field, singing a ballad.*

DIANA [*to the tune of "Someday My Prince Will Come"*]: Someday, my prince will come / Then nobody will call me dumb...
[*Segue to "Who Am I Anyway?" from A Chorus Line*] Who am I anyway? / I don't have a résumé ...
[*Enter PRINCE CHARLES. He takes her in his arms.*]

CHARLES [*to the tune of "You Are the Sunshine of My Life"*]: You are the one to be my wife / Except when Camilla and I are aloooone / You are the apple of my eye / Bear me an heir, Princess Diiiii.

## ACT II: THE PALACE

*In the palace, Diana is surrounded by the* CHORUS/PAPARAZZI *as she sobs into a bucket.*

CHORUS [*to the tune of "Money, Money" from Cabaret*]: Tabloids make the world go 'round / The world go 'round / The world go 'round / Tabloids make the world go 'round / That clinking, clanking sound / When you we've found!...
DIANA [*to the tune of "Food Glorious Food"*]: Moods, glorious moods / I suffer from them / Food glorious food / Bad for a fatale femme / Think I'll throw myself down the stairs / Now I've finally produced those heirs...
CHORUS [*to the tune of "Every Breath You Take" by The Police*]: Every step you take / Every move you make / We'll be watching you.
DIANA: Can't you see / What you've done to me? / My poor heart aches / Why don't you jump in the lake? / I'm as thin as a rake / You all think I'm a flake / My picture you take / I think I'll have a piece of cake / I'll be watching you.
[*Enter* PRINCE CHARLES.]
CHARLES [*to the tune of "God Save the Queen"*]: My mummy is the Queen / Please don't upset the Queen / I love Camilla / Camilla is glorious / Camilla is victorious / Please don't be notorious / God save the Queen.
DIANA [*to Olivia Newton-John's "I Honestly Love You"*] I hate you / I honestly hate you...

## ACT III: AFTER THE FUNERAL

The CHORUS/PAPARAZZI *gather around Diana's grave.*

CHORUS [*to "Who's Sorry Now"*]: Who's sorry now? / Who's sorry now? / Whose heart is breaking / Now we've killed our cash cow? [*As they bow their heads in regret,* DIANA *mysteriously reappears to them as a vision.*]
DIANA [*to the tune of "Don't Cry for Me Argentina"*]: Don't cry for me, Great Britain / You know you always snubbed me / All through my wild times / When I was a young girl / And now you're sorry? / Well, you can shove it...

[*Curtain.*]

# Film People Are Super Special!

Theatre People may be special, but Film People are Super Special!

You can always tell if you're talking to a Film Person by the way they respond to the query, "...And what is it that you do for a living?" A not-so-special, say, secretary or brain surgeon will respond, "Why, I am a brain surgeon" or "I am a secretary." And a Theatre Person will say, "I do Theatre," and then retort defensively, "What is it that *you* do?"

A Film Person will first of all give you a look like, "You don't know, do you? Right? Really, you're kidding? You really don't know what I do?" Then, after bowing their head for a moment, as if silently asking the Gods to one day relieve you of your woeful ignorance, they will look you straight in the eye, the same way, say, Jane Fonda looked at Donald Sutherlad in *Klute,* and say, "I'm into...[pause for effect]...film."

Film People have a way of saying they're "into" film that is reminiscent of an accountant saying, "I'm 'into' bondage" or Uma Thurman saying, "I'm 'into' cigars." Film People are into film the way Moonies are into Krishna; Theatre People do theatre the way a prostitute does a John; and the rest of us are just extras in this low-budget movie called Life.

Film People are Super Special because, unlike Theatre People, who are just plain special, they are privileged to work in a medium that they consider to be a synthesis of all the arts. A Film Person, therefore, is not just a writer, not just a musician, not just an artist, not just a businessman, but a super special blend of all these talents and more! This is why if you ask a Film Person how they are doing, they will inevitably reply, "I'm super busy these days." Too super-busy to read newspapers, listen to music, look at art or watch any movie other than their own over and over again. Which is why sometimes you find yourself coming out of so many movies — especially during the Toronto International Film Festival — saying, "Wow! That was super boring!"

Film is a time-based medium that is not grounded in the immediacy of reality, and the same can be said of Film People. That is why you can be sitting in Toronto on a nice sunny day, and a Film Person will look up at you and tell you what time it is in LA. The fact that a Film Person can do this is part of the "magic" of being "into...film."

Film People, especially editors, directors and people who write about film, are also always "super tired". This is because they are on their feet all day, standing in line to get into a film. It is also because Film People, unlike ordinary people, sit through hours and hours of condensed time. When you think that each movie is essentially a lifetime of events compressed into a two-hour format, and that each Film Person has lived several lives over, Film People have, through the process of watching many films, acquired the Wisdom of the Ancients — of *Porky's*, *Police Academy III* and *Twilight Zone: The Movie*. Film People are mentally and emotionally very, very old.

Film People are fond of telling you that Film People are gypsies. When they tell you this, they are giving you an important insight into both their professional and personal lives. Film People are unable to sustain relationships with other human beings simply because the nature of their business compels them to migrate from set to set in search of food.

If you're not sure if you're talking to a Film Person, there are certain words and key phrases that tip you off that you are actually talking to the real thing, even if that person appears at first to be merely an usher taking tickets at the Uptown movie theatre. One of these key phrases is, "I want to make a low-budget feature film with a small crew and cast...just like Roger Corman." Another heard lately in corporate welfare-deprived Ontario is, "I think I'll move to Halifax." Other key words to listen for are "Telefilm," "flat-bed", "option", "free booze" and, of course, "super", as in, "Wasn't that film super?"

Beware of mistaking someone wearing a plastic pass on a cord around their neck for a real Film Person. Often these so-called Film People, who you frequently see at the Toronto International Film Festival, are truck drivers, bookstore owners, leeches, hangers-on, journalists, investors and other wackos and scum.

Another way to distinguish a real Film Person from a flibbertigibbet just prentending to be a Film Person is by their complete and utter contempt for writers. If you introduce yourself as a writer to a Film Person, they will automatically crane their necks and look around for somebody else in the room to talk to, or tell you that old joke about who the Polish actress had sex with (hint: it wasn't a Film Person). This time-honoured, super special, super politically incorrect joke is ironic from a group of people who, odiously enough, are also fond of telling you, "The book was much, much better than the movie," even though they were too super busy to read it.

# I Am Curious Celadon

There we were, sixteen of the most talented people in the country, sitting around my kitchen table. It was hard to believe, but we were all flat broke. It soon became clear that we had no other recourse: it was time to make a porn film.

There is no shame in making a porn film, we told ourselves. This country has a tradition of pornographic filmmaking as great as documentary filmmaking. (Without those early porn films, certain Canadian movie moguls would not have been able to finance the film distribution empires that they operate today.) In the olden days, an "art film from Montreal" was a synonym for a skin flick. By making our first porn film, we would just be getting in touch with our cultural roots. As an added bonus, it meant that all of the women in the room could display their ample bosoms for artistic reasons, as opposed to the usual political or medical ones.

Since most of us were used to writing and directing short operettas, witty bedroom farces or mildly amusing, award-winning short films, we decided to do some research. We studied our market carefully by holding a marathon screening of the 120 or so most popular porn videos that I rented at the local Nipa Hut. We decided that what we needed was a classic stud, similar to the ones that appeared in all of these videos: an aging, rotund, hairy guy with mean black eyes. This would be the atypical short-fingered vulgarian who would appear repeatedly in our pornos in his different guises: the health club owner, the nightclub owner, the meter reader, the milkman, whatever. One of us immediately proceeded down to College Street and returned after a few minutes with a gentleman who fit this description, right down to the desired ruff of black hair that furled out from beneath his shirt collar.

Our second challenge was to find an actor who would be willing to take her clothes off. One quick phone call to ACTRA and we found exactly who we were looking for: a short, stocky, peroxided blond, with a nose that had been surgically fashioned into a ski jump, so she resembled a friendly, beige-coloured Pekingese (a Pekingese that had trained at the National Theatre School). A method actor who had once sat in the same room where Stanislavski once spoke, she showed up immediately on our doorstep dressed instinctively in the appropriate attire: a muscle shirt, satin boxer shorts, bobby socks and patent leather high heels.

Satisfied with our casting choices, we then set about finding the perfect location, which — given what we had seen while doing our research — meant a bedroom with more lights than your average operating theatre. In every porn film we had seen, it seemed aesthetically essential that the actors cast confusing cross-shadows on the walls. It was also *de rigueur* to have a huge double bed, above which hung a bad artist's pastel rendering of a Palm Beach motel. Luckily, my bedroom was perfect.

After hours of debate, story-editing and consultation about what should actually be the story, we decided to throw narrative out the window and begin the conflict with "*A scantily clad* WOMAN *lies on the* BED. *A* MAN *enters.*" At this point, the actress asked us what her motivation was and all sixteen of us, like true Hollywood producers, screamed, "Money! Heh, heh, heh. That's your motivation." Then we split into small conversational groups and said things like, "Actors are cattle."

At the point, however, when MAN was about to *Enter*, all sixteen of us (being the sensitive, artistic souls that we are) simultaneously turned away and burst into tears. It seems that we had created a scenario so tender, so touching, so sensitive and human that we could not even bear to watch our own handiwork, as MAN tenderly ran his vulgar short fingers through WOMAN's bright yellow, candy-floss-coloured hair. It was just too beautiful.

The room filled with the sound of sobbing as each of us remembered that special moment in our lives, sometime in the mid-eighties, when we, too, were allowed to have the kind of sex we were about to depict — sex without concern, without care, without censorship, without love. The kind of sex that two rhinoceroses might have naturally on the banks of a river.

Overcome, we yelled, "CUT!" But even though we told them they'd no longer be paid, the couple on the bed just kept on mating, unbroken by the burden of memory, while we looked on in horror. The very worst thing in the world had happened: they were in love. And, despite our best intentions, we had managed to make another sensitive, artistic, crappy Canadian art film after all.

# Authors Are Wonderful People!

If Theatre People are "special" and Film People are "super special", then what, I ask you, is an author? Why, an author, of course, is simply…wonderful!

Every year I, like the rest of the city, look forward to autumn, when hundreds of simply wonderful authors fall from the bus platforms onto the streets of Toronto in search of a clean T-shirt, a decent cup of decaffeinated mochaccino and the Harbourfront International Festival of Authors. The way the authors change colour every year, from green to red to silvery white, after a brief jealous stint in an airless auditorium listening to a more well-known author read; the requisite overindulgence in taco chips and spicy salsa that follows each event; the aftermath of hangovers from too much donated white wine that rarely has an alcohol content above 8 per cent — this is one of Canada's greatest natural spectacles!

Of course, at the International Festival of Authors there are so many people walking around masquerading as authors it may be difficult for you to discern a real author from someone who makes a living writing every second page of the Canadian Tire catalogue. Appearances can be deceiving, as every single person at the festival not only will be sporting a thick pair of bookish spectacles but also will claim to be "working on a book". One way to weed out the real literati from those who pretend to write is, when they tell you they are "working on a book," to promptly respond, "Oh, really? Who by?" If they answer with a name other than their own, then you can be assured that you are not actually talking to a glamorous, well-known author but rather a mere lowly editor, publisher, publicist, critic, proofreader or bookstore owner. Sometimes when people say they are "working on a book", what they mean is that they are struggling to get through the thing. And sometimes they mean that they always meant to write a book one day, after they get that pesky cost-of-living thing figured out.

Another way to spot the real author in the room is to look for the individual with the red, kidney-shaped dents on their upper nose, repeatedly winking, blinking, bumping into things and rubbing their eyes. This would be a real author, usually a first-time-published writer who has worn contact lenses in anticipation of having their picture taken by the paparazzi. Older authors, who have had many novels published, have cried so many tears at the frustration of trying to collect royalties that their tear ducts have dried up and they are unable to wear contact lenses any more.

But what exactly is it, you ask, that makes an author so wonderful? An author, first of all, is different from an ordinary person because he or she has already expressed everything on paper that they have to tell the world. Therefore, an author does not have to engage in actual conversation, unless they need to go to the bathroom, to eat something or to hail a taxi to their hotel. Isn't that wonderful? Such purity! Such economy of human interaction. But deprive a famous author of their publicist — or the constant, kind, attentive presence of Greg Gatenby — and you will see them panic.

However, if you really want to get a rise out of an author, politely tell him or her that you have not read their last book and have no idea what it's about, but that you think that he or she is a "simply wonderful person." Most authors, having triumphed over bad childhoods, cannot handle the concept of "unconditional love", which is why they started writing tall tales (professionally lying)in the first place. This is why the bookstores are overstocked with "coming-of-age tales" written by first-time novelists trying to improve their bad reality.

So if you really want to get a reaction out of writers, tell them that you think they are "just wonderful." They will roll their eyes, look at you suspiciously, shake their heads in confusion or even turn an interesting colour right in front of you — anything but admit that you could be right. This comes not from modesty, but from the deep-seated insecurity that drives them to be morally superior commentators on the absurdity of our society. Any author worth their salsa, chips and cheap glass of wine will deny their own wonderfulness and steer you in the direction of the nearest bookstore. Soon you will find yourself spending wonderful moments alone with the author in bed…reading their book. Intimacy without actual personal contact? What could be more wonderful or nineties than that?

## You Know It's Time To Quit The Band When…

- The last time you got "good press" was at the dry cleaners.
- Girls spraypaint "Give Up!", rather than their names, on your amps.
- Your bass player has hair down to his waist, but the top of his head has one of those mysterious crop circles.
- The first few bars of every new song you play sound suspiciously like "Surfin' U.S.A."
- Artistically, you're still trying to achieve that New Wave/Kraftwerk sound.
- Your girlfriend keeps referring to your career as "your therapy sessions".
- There's another band with the same name as you with a number one hit song playing in the United States.
- You've always performed "unplugged", so you don't understand why it's so special when other performers do.
- Whenever you play in a bar, people refuse to turn off the juke box…in fact, they turn it up.
- Every time you play, people take over the microphone, trying to join in on the karaoke.
- Your lead singer ends every set with his imitation of an epileptic seizure, and an ambulance actually arrives.
- You had to get a job at Long and McQuade to pay off what you owe them in back equipment rental.
- Your bass player has so much brain damage from doing drugs that he's afraid to go onstage because the electrical cords look like snakes.
- One day, when you're eating your Alpha-Bits, the letters mysteriously swirl around to spell "Quit The Band!"

• Your leather pants don't fit you anymore.
• The last time you dove into the audience, you broke your hip because there was nobody there to land on.
• Your lead singer opens every set with that same corny old line: "Whatever happened to Reuben Kincaid?"
• After you play your first song, the audience starts yelling, "Bring back the bad stand-up comedian!"
• Your parents tell you that they really enjoy your music.
• No one in your band has been laid for three years.
• Every time you and the guys get together to write a new song, you end up passed out in front of the TV watching *Three's Company*.
• You become so traumatized and jaded that the only music you find relaxing now is Burt Bacharach's Greatest Hits.
• You don't smash your guitars at the end of every set anymore because "its too expensive."
• Your lead singer catches pneumonia after pretending to give head to a germ-laden microphone.
• When the fog machine is turned on you all start coughing.
• The biggest city you've ever played is Estevan, Saskatchewan.
• Your manager advises you that you would sound much better if you would underlay your tracks with the sound of whales mating.
• No one ever asks you to play a benefit for fear that nobody will show up and all the children will starve.
• Your lead singer puts a condom on the microphone so he won't catch pneumonia again.
• Every time you go to a used record store, there are fifty copies of your indie album sitting there, many of them signed by you to your friends.
• Even though the name of your band only has three letters in it, the press constantly misspells it.
• You finally get that big gig on *Breakfast Television* but are bumped by a troupe of ten-year old Scottish sword dancers wearing kilts.
• Pamela Des Barres shows up at the backstage door and tells you that she's your "biggest fan".
• It's been so long since you last played that a family of muskrats have built a nest inside your amp.

• You can't even get a gig at a bar mitzvah.

• You have to write the lyrics to your own songs on your arm because you've forgotten them since the last time you played.

• You can't pogo any more without the flaps of fat at your waistline making a clapping sound.

• Every waking moment of your day is accompanied by a high, tinny sound whining in your ears.

• You're still playing the guitar your Mom bought for you at Simpson's Sears.

• The whole band gets together regularly to drink a few brews and mourn the death of Keith Moon.

• You drink two beers and you're in bed with a hangover for the next four days.

• Your lead singer sits you all down for an honest talk, telling you how he wants to get a job, buy a house and have a kid, like a normal person for a change.

• Your lead singer takes a vow of silence and joins a Buddhist cult.

• You are invited to be a guest on *Jerry Springer*, but the subject is "People who want to be rock stars but are fifty years old and still practising in their Moms' basements".

• Your kids are embarassed because you look like Fonzie in your leather jacket.

• No one in the band wants to play past ten at night because they get too tired.

• Your drummer has been dead for three years and you just noticed.

• Instead of a toke or a drink or a hit, people offer you a swig of Geritol before you go on.

• "I'm living on dog food" is more than just a lyric for you — it's the truth.


# Bad Restaurant Decor

The cultural anthropologist in me has always been fascinated by Bad Restaurant Decor. True Bad Restaurant Decor is getting harder to find these days, what with most people's hyper-awareness of "kitsch". True Bad Restaurant Decor is not something that can be curated — it is something that one accidentally stumbles across. You know you are truly experiencing Bad Restaurant Decor when you are sitting in a little diner near Algonquin Park, about to bite into your $2 cheeseburger, and your eye alights on a painting on a distant wall. The subject is a snowy, cloud-cloaked mountain peak rendered in icy, aqueous tones of blue and green. It looks like a still from a Leni Riefenstahl film, but here you are eating a hamburger in Algonquin Park. The mountain peak has nothing to do with your immediate experience. The nearest mountain peak is thousands of miles away in Alberta. It is an example of True Bad Restaurant Decor.

True Bad Restaurant Decor makes you wonder why it is there in the first place. For instance, if the little diner is near Algonquin Park, would it not make more sense to have one of those Group of Seven knock-offs on the wall instead of this snowy European mountain peak? Perhaps something a little more indigenous to the area, such as a slightly off-register reproduction of Tom Thomson's lone, twisted jack pine would be more appropriate — c'mon, you all know the one. You've seen it a thousand times, hanging in dentists' offices and taking up space on postcard racks.

How about a glossy photograph of deer drinking from a lake — its surface starry with camera glare — showcased behind plastic in an aluminum frame? Or perhaps a picture of some actual food, as we *are* in a restaurant? There's where that old fire-engine red Coca-Cola poster (the Real Thing reproduced a million times) comes in handy.

There's always that hyper-realist painting of the silver, streamlined, 1950s New York diner, illuminated by a single streetlight, which Toronto restaurant owners seem to be particularly fond of, along with the black-and-white photo of James Dean walking along the Boulevard of Broken Dreams. There's nothing that adds more to the enjoyment of a bagel in one of Toronto's many coffee houses than the opportunity to have a momentary identification with a Hollywood icon symbolizing teenage angst. Except for a Hollywood icon that symbolizes your eclectic good taste in second-run movies, as is signified by the redundant image of Humphrey Bogart.

Some restaurant decor is meant to lead you to believe that you are having a dining experience in another time or place. A poster of the Moulin Rouge by Toulouse-Lautrec is, on a certain level, intended to transport you to a charming, absinthe-ridden café in 1920s Paris. Likewise, a painting of the Last Supper in one of its mottled paint-by-numbers or mirrored versions hanging on a restaurant wall can transport you to 33 A.D. and remind you that you are always, in a way, "breaking bread with Christ".

However, back to the mountain peak. True Bad Restaurant Decor should be slightly postmodern, the equivalent of, say, accidentally finding a shiny, wet seashell in the middle of a desert or a diamond in the middle of a cow-pie. When I find myself distracted by a piece of Bad Restaurant Decor, I find myself wondering about the perversity of the mind that put it there. I always want to ask, "Why did you choose this picture of a snowy-breasted mountain top, as opposed to, say, a picture of a romantic young girl playing the piano or naked children warming their hands in front of the fire?" But I never do. That would spoil the magic. As bad as Bad Restaurant Decor may be, it is still a representation of the owner's soul.

Bad Restaurant Decor cannot be created for you by a team of designers. A room full of hip, carefully chosen examples of kitsch doesn't do it for me, so it cannot be found on the walls of trendy, big-city establishments. It can, however, be found on the walls of any Red Lobster, McDonald's or any older restaurant.

Bad art has no theme or purpose. It exists solely to facilitate your next epiphany. There is plenty of bad art in Toronto. You don't even have to look for it. It will eventually find your eyes…if they're open.

# Mrs. 666 Is Ready to See You Now...

# Ten Short, Short Stories About Toronto (All True!)

Once I was at a party at the Art Gallery of Ontario. I lost the gold cross that was hanging from my neck. I went over to the buffet where Kaspar, an art dealer friend of mine, was selecting an oyster from a bucket of ice. Kaspar pried open the oyster and the gold cross was inside.

A long time ago, my friend James and I were sitting on the sunny back stoop of the building where he lived on Liberty Street. We were eating peaches. After we finished the peaches, we casually threw the stones onto the gravel driveway. Several years later, after not seeing each other for a long time, we were sitting on the same stoop admiring a pretty tree, laden with fruit, growing in the driveway. We looked at the tree, then at each other, and went, "Hey! Wait a minute!"

I was in the middle of writing a script, and in one of the scenes the heroine throws a big, shiny engagement ring over Niagara Falls. The writing wasn't going well, so I decided to take a shortcut up a back alley to a restaurant and get a take-out cup of coffee. On my way to the restaurant, something shiny burried in the gravel of the alley caught my eye. I scraped at it with my foot and found an oversized, shiny engagement ring, the size of a woman's bracelet, with a plastic diamond as big as my fist.

My friend Jennifer decided one day that she would tell my fortune using an ordinary pack of playing cards. She asked me to pull a card from the deck and turn it over. It was the queen of diamonds. She told me that was "my card". The next day, we were walking together along Bay Street, and lying on the sidewalk before us was a single playing card, face down. I picked up the card and turned it over — it was the queen of diamonds.

About ten years ago, I was sitting in the celebrity laundromat at Spadina and Queen, writing a poem in my notebook about fish. Suddenly the door to the laundromat swung open, and a man came in carrying a chain from which hung six large fish. He dropped the fish inside a washing machine, started it up, and then, without saying a word or meeting anybody's eyes, he left. I never finished the poem.

Last year my friend P., a brilliant yet impoverished director and actor, thought he would try to declare bankruptcy. Then he found out it costs $200 to declare bankruptcy. He just couldn't afford it.

On September 29, 1989, my boyfriend — after sharing a single futon with me for two years in a tiny room in the Cameron Hotel — suddenly decided that he would leave me for good. He told me he was just going to the store for a minute and that he would be right back. I never saw him again. He never even returned to claim his clothes, shoes or personal belongings. Months went by, and even though I was glad he was finally out of my life, I found myself wishing that I could just see his face again — just one more time. One night I was in the back room of The Rivoli, and Carson, the bartender, told me he'd found something on the floor when he was cleaning up. He presented me with a July 1990 Metropass — with my boyfriend's face grinning merrily up at me.

My friend Kareen always told me it was bad luck to see an albino animal. In the same week in the fall of 1985, I saw an albino squirrel and my friend Mindy and I saw an albino praying mantis lying on the sidewalk on Niagara Street. The day we found the praying mantis, I woke up in the middle of the night, full of anxiety and not feeling very well. In the darkness of the room, I could make out an eerie white shape perched on my desk. It turned out to be my neighbour's albino cat, which I had no idea she even owned. I threw a book at the cat, but it didn't move. (It turns out albino cats are also deaf mutes.) Within a week, I was in the hospital, deathly ill with encephalitis, a disease that makes it difficult for you to speak or understand what others are saying. Four months later, when I had finally recovered, my neighbour came to the door and tearfully told me her cat had died of mysterious causes.

A couple of years ago, I was at a very late party for Annie Sprinkle in the Spadina Hotel. I lost my "Lucky Watch" — a men's mod watch with baroque hands and a patent leather strap. I was heartbroken. I never took that watch off my wrist. The next day at 9 a.m., I went to the Shadowshows office to have a meeting with Colin. He had not been at the party, but Colin immediately presented me with the missing "Lucky Watch". That morning, Jeremy, the man who had found the watch, had coincidentally brought it to the Shadowshows office for Colin to admire.

A couple of years ago on a summer day, I was walking my friend's dogs down by Cherry Beach. Suddenly, out of the weeds emerged a cloud of monarch butterflies. There were so many the bright day seemed suddenly cloudy. The dogs went wild and we started running to get away from the swarm of butterflies that spiralled up into the sky and then dissipated. Moments later, there wasn't a single butterfly in sight. Later that evening, my friend Robin dropped by my house in Parkdale to show me the drawings in her book. Scotch-taped inside the pages was a single dead monarch butterfly.

## Lust at Loblaws

We were looking for a Vanilla Bean. Not Vanilla Extract or, God forbid, Imitation Vanilla Extract — which are both, as far as we're concerned, a homeless baker's equivalent of a bottle of bitters ("Excuse me, kind sir, but may I please have a quarter to whip up a crème brûlée?") — but a real Vanilla Bean. A real Vanilla Bean is a blood-brown filament that resembles a dried snake's tongue. It is packaged in its own test tube, which attests to its scientifically proven powers to make even Superman strip off his tights and yell,

"Take me, I'm yours!" at the first hint of its subtle aroma stewing slyly in a pot of oatmeal and apples.

My friend M.'s insistence on having a real Vanilla Bean led us to Dupont and Christie where we found, like a Casa Loma amongst corner-store fruit stands, the "new" Loblaws, with its smart brick and green metal facade. Who knew that our search for vanilla would lead us into an orgiastic embarrassment of riches, a cornucopia of colours, sights and sounds? Who knew that a Loblaws, for Christ's sake, could actually make love to you — could provide you with such a tactile, visceral, completely sensuous experience that afterwards you just had to go home and have a nap?

At the door, a gasp of refreshing cold air greeted our hot, tired bodies. In the entrance was not the usual bubble-gum machine or automatic horsey, but an in-store travel agency inviting us to expand our horizons by visiting Greece or Bali. We moved on into a maze of books. *Home Cookin' With Dave Letterman's Mom* and *Heart Smart Chinese Cooking* lent us more food for thought. Then our savage breasts were soothed by the sight of $4.99 tape compilations: The Tragically Hip, The Who and Trooper; and our minds felt massaged by the masterful fingertips of Marshall McLuhan himself as we spied *Cherry 2000* and Pope John Paul II on the same video rack.

The store then lured us into a corner known as the Flower Market, a literal Eden filled with all of the diversity Mother Nature has to offer — flocks of bird of paradise and gaggles of gladioli nestled among stars of Bethlehem, bunches of lavender and pots of African violets. The dew of lilies and orchids glistened on the icy tombs of glass, and arid bunches of roses dried in their nooses of shiny ribbon.

We proceeded down the first aisle, Frozen Foods, where clouds of vapour swirled mysteriously about our ankles, and tubs of wild blueberries, exotic fruit pies and twenty-six different kinds of butter beckoned. It was here that M. announced, after disappearing momentarily into the mist, that each grocery item came with a digital display that told you, with one touch of a finger, the cost per 100 grams.

We moved towards the In-store Bakery, which featured a Band of Merry Bakers placing and replacing custard tarts and cakes adorned with sugar-shellacked strawberries and kiwis, in a pastry case filled with frosted chocolate logs and cream-filled tortes. The witch in "Hansel and Gretel" could have built a thirty-unit condo with the sugary supplies we found in those bins — Sticky Toffee Puddings, Mississippi Mud Pies, Petit Fours, Chocolate Truffles, Meringue Nests and cans and cans of grout-like Devon Custard Cream.

Pretzels, cinnamon buns, croissants and perversely large bagels with exotic titles, like chocolate chip, pesto, cheddar-herb and sun-dried tomato, lay steps away from the slabs of Black Angus beef, sweating beneath their tight plastic wrap, next to the kosher turkeys and pale slivers of tender white veal...

After a few minutes of examining the comforting images of childhood on a package of Lipton's Tea called "Snow Angels", I realized that both M. and I had, like James Bond in a brothel, become distracted from our mission — which was, as you recall, to find a real Vanilla Bean. I found M. gazing in wonder at a selection of de-alcoholized French and German wines, such as PC Memories of Champagne. After being momentarily riveted by a selection of Quaker Oats Low-Fat Rice Cakes in Cinnamon Bun, Caramel Corn and Butter Popcorn flavours, I tracked her down again in the "ethnic" aisle, examining bottles of Coconut Gel, Jackfruit and Palm Fruit.

I carefully led M. past cheap, attractive kitchen gadgets bobbing strategically at impulse-shopping eye level, past the section of twenty different Dijon mustards, past the four-can pack of Clover Leaf salmon wrapped in its own net, past the wicker lawn furniture, past the Club Aisle with its 10-litre bottles of Fleecy and 10-pound carton of Pepperidge Farm Goldfish crackers, towards an atrium where I thought there might be an exit, an escape from Loblaws' smothering hold. Instead we were confronted by an area that resembled a kind of barn, where...

Scores of Voortman cookies lay stacked like coins, and piles of curly cappelletti pasta gleamed like seashells in plastic bins;

mackerel and smoked rainbow trout glittered on ice among gleaming slivers of smelt; peppers the colour of Crayola crayons competed for attention with kohlrabies the size of 1950s fabulous lamp fixtures, plums the size of dinosaur eggs, cherimoyas the size of pine cones and mountains of portobello mushrooms with tops big enough to easily seat a caterpillar smoking from a hookah waiting to enchant us.

Exhausted, but strangely satiated without having bought a single thing, M. and I made our way to the exit, past the Mövenpick Rotisserie's daily chicken special, where M. finally recovered the presence of mind to ask an employee if they had Vanilla Beans.

"No, but I wish we did."

We walked out, fulfilled but not full, into the sweet summer sunshine, the strains of Joni Mitchell's "Big Yellow Taxi" still singing in our heads. No, we did not find a Vanilla Bean. We had something better than a Vanilla Bean — invigoration, a renewed sense of spirit, a just-been-to-the-spa-like confidence in the world that only those who have been loved, even if it is by a Loblaws, could ever know.

# Apocalypse Fever!

Last week, I was relaxing on the big, old pink mattress in my living room — the "life raft" as I affectionately refer to it, awash as it is in a sea of old *Allure* magazines and discarded Vantage cigarette packages, in whose mysterious folds is hidden everything that I need to survive (my non-child-proof lighter, the TV remote) — reading a tacky magazine and watching the Shopping Channel at the same time. Now, you can read a tacky magazine by itself or watch the Shopping Channel by itself, but the two activities complement each other, the way an expensive brie can complement a fine wine that may have tasted too acidic on its own. Anyway, as I was pushing away one of the many overly affectionate, drooling cats who were, like drowning men, trying desperately to clamber aboard my cozy floating Holiday Oasis, an alarming scenario began to unfold on TV, one that confirmed my suspicion that the end of the world is nigh — no, indeed, it is already here!

The last time I looked, two friendly, gender-complementary hosts had been exchanging typically witty *Sonny and Cher*-type repartee over plastic baggies of homemade potpourri, produced for only pennies from out of the mysterious amber chambers of the Ronco Food Dehydrator, $29.95. Now the program had taken on a more menacing tone. The female host was somberly holding up a baggie of dried apricots and talking about how the apocalypse could be on our doorstep, and how it was important to be prepared in case of an emergency or a sudden natural disaster. The male host nodded and cited recent blizzards that had shut down the US midwest, parts of the coast and most of Europe as being evidence that, indeed, the predictions of Nostradamus were at last coming true — that in the last few years, because of flood, fire and riots, many people had found themselves without water or food.

In fact, the female host suggested, it would not be wise to be without a Ronco Food Dehydrator in the event of a sudden holocaust or complete collapse of the world economy. While the other unprepared chipmunks wandered the streets, looting and killing in desperate search of food, you could be happily squirrelled away in your home, eating bags and bags of delicious beef jerky and dehydrated pineapple.

The male host added brightly, "If you do happen to find yourself trapped in your car when the big flood hits, cold and scared because hypothermia is setting in — and perhaps you find yourself not thinking so straight, as people do when their adrenaline glands are really pumping — you will be grateful that you had the foresight to stow a baggie of delicious dried apricots in your glove compartment to provide you with quick food energy." But, as the wall of water rushes towards your windshield, you are perhaps not so grateful that you have chosen a baggie of dried apricots as your last meal.

At the same time, I happened to be reading an article in the tabloid *Sun* revealing the "Third Prophecy of the Virgin Mary".

This prophecy, given to two Portuguese children near the town of Fátima by an apparition of the Virgin in 1917, was considered so terrifying and gruesome that it has been shrouded in papal secrecy — that is, until the reporters at the *Sun* bribed a ninety-year-old priest into revealing the content of the text. The prophecy tells of a nuclear holocaust scheduled to happen sometime before the year 2000 in which "millions and millions will die from hour to hour and the living will envy the dead." The present pope, after taking a privileged peek at the famous Scroll of Fatima, was rumoured to have emerged from his chambers, shaking his head and crying, "Poor Canada…poor, poor Canada."

Canada? I thought this was all supposed to happen in LA!

So, I found myself thinking that the end of the world really is coming. Even the Ronco Food Dehydrator people know. It's too bad I maxed out my credit card at Christmas because I really should be stocking up on supplies — powdered milk, bottled water, Science Diet and MAC's lip liner in Spice. I suppose I should also make sure I have a spare set of spectacles, so I don't end up like Piggy in *Lord of the Flies*, wandering around blind, bellowing, "Where's the conch?" while my so-called friends steal my food and throw rocks at me.

I suppose I should also learn to drive and get a goat, a gun, some chickens and a piece of land on high ground. And a medical kit — no, better yet, marry a doctor, quick — a shortwave radio and an emergency supply of Q-tips. And I had better be prepared, in this new cashless society, to barter my services (I hope that doesn't mean what I think it traditionally means) in exchange for goods.

Remember, in the end, whichever side owns the most Ronco Food Dehydrators wins. The rest of us will be cowering in terror with our cats, nibbling on bits of leftover chocolate we got for Christmas. Yes, the millennium is coming, but I won't have to worry because I just got a letter from Ed McMahon that says, "MS. DONNA LYPCHUCK, YOU'VE FINALLY MADE IT! YOUR $11,000,000 PRIZE IS GUARANTEED." Imagine how many Ronco Food Dehydrators I'll buy with that. Thanks, Ed.

As for the rest of you, consider yourselves forewarned.

# Bogus Queen Street Lard Butts on Parade

OK, this Bogus Queen Street Lard Butts on Parade thing ACTUALLY started last summer. One sunny morning, Fluffy, Equestrian Girl, Gerald the D.O.P. and myself were sitting on the patio of The 360, one of the places where you can get a really good view of the Bogus Queen Street Lard Butts passing by — or just walking back and forth every five minutes, doing their version of the Queen Street Strut on the little stretch between Soho and Spadina, showing off, wearing the clothes, the shades…you know.

Anyway, all of us were really tired and really hungry, and we've all lived on Queen Street for something like fifteen years and consider ourselves to be the real, authentic Queen Streeters, even though most of the time we don't look like, say, a *Liberty Street* writer's conception of a what a Queen Streeter looks like. We dropped all that pseudo-vampire, rockabilly, leather-chaps, black-eyeliner, purple-hair-polish, laddered-tights, kooky-vintage thing you get into in, like, 1981 — or, if you live in Vancouver, now — *ages ago.*

Anyway, we're sitting there, and we're all in the same kind of rare bad mood that happens only when you've been drinking the night before and your blood sugar is really, really low and all you want to do is eat something really yang and salty like a plate of greasy bacon and eggs like you get at the Stem, only you can't even get into the Stem on a Sunday because the line-up is too long. I mean, it's not like Elvis is in the building or anything. It's just a nice little greasy spoon run by Bill and Frieda at the corner of Queen and Spadina, and a nice place to go for a fast, cheap meal *if you can get in.*

Anyway, we're sitting outside at The 360 — where we ended up because we were too tired to walk past Bathurst to either the Future Bakery or La Hacienda and wait at those places for hours to be served (it only really happens on a Sunday) — looking at the menu, trying to decide what to eat, fast, before the chef takes off suddenly for the day, like he sometimes does, and Equestrian Girl is whining about how there are no bacon and eggs on the menu because she's feeling really yin, and the waitress snaps at her, "If you want bacon and eggs, go to the Stem!" And, of course, we can't go to the Stem because we can't get by all the baby carriages, briefcases, rollerblades and 5-foot-wide sunhats that are in there.

And then Gerald looks around and states, really matter-of-factly, "We're surrounded by idiots." Sure enough, we look at the crowds of people sashaying past, and yeah, the people walking down the street, in gangs of five abreast, shoulder-to-shoulder, like the cast of the cartoon *Hercules,* *do* look really weird in their platform shoes, thigh-high knee socks, bras and not much else. And then a dogfight breaks out between two pitbulls, a woman walks by pushing a baby carriage full of the Dionne Quintuplets and two guys fighting over the parking space right in front of The 360 start yelling and pushing each other, and everybody on the patio starts yelling, "Shut up!" Another guy comes down the street juggling three sticks in the air and Equestrian Girl — who has had her head buried in the menu to this point — looks around, sees a gang of ten extremely heavy girls, wearing tights and bras and little else, and says, "They are all lard butts. These people are nothing but Bogus Queen Street Lard Butts on Parade."

Now, I know this is kind of a vicious statement, but for some reason it has sort of stuck with me. I like the sound of it — Bogus Queen Street Lard Butts on Parade. (As opposed to, I guess, our Authentic Queen Street Lard Butts on Parade.) I kind of hate those people, too, who go on — like I'm about to — about the good old days on Queen Street, but I can remember when there was nothing but tumbleweeds blowing down that little stretch of the street, and the only place you could go to allay your loneliness on a Sunday was the old marble bar at the Peter Pan. That was in the days before there was a Rivoli or a BamBoo or even a Cameron Hotel.

Now it's like the inside of the Eaton Centre out there, what with Ralph Lauren's present to Queen Street, Club Monaco ("There goes the neighbourhood," we said when we saw that thing all wrapped up in its big red bow), the Body Shop, Guess, Roots and HMV, and all those people, walking up and down the street with that "look" on their faces — you know, like they're *looking* for somebody. My friend Troy said it was the first thing he noticed when he moved here from Vancouver, that people on Queen Street always seem to be looking for "something" spiritual or "someone" who can change their lives. It's true. I hope they find it in Aldo.

Anyway, the funniest thing I've seen on Queen Street lately is this wild-haired guy doing a kind of Jim-Morrison-wandering-in-the-desert version of the Queen Street Strut, wearing black silk jeans, his long, black chiffon shirt blowing open to expose his carotene-coloured chest. He moved slowly, like an altar boy approaching the altar, a beatific yet benevolent smile on his face, as if he had found that "something" sitting inside the cage of the Rivoli patio. His attitude was so reverent, so "follow me", that myself and the group of strangers passing by just cracked right up.

So if you see me strutting my Bogus Old Queen Street Lard Butt up and down the street, remember that I, too, am on a quest for something — a good place to read the paper and eat breakfast without too much barking, crying, minding the GAP or tourists asking me for directions to Queen Street.

You want to know how to find Queen Street? Just follow the Easter Parade.

# A Gambler's Life

I'm not much of gambler, but I've gone out with guys who were. You know, the kind of guy who makes you start humming, "He's an ambler, a gambler, a midnight rambler," just at the sight of him — jean jacket, black cowboy boots, a beer clenched in each fist. The kind of guy who will try to teach you how to play pool, then roll his eyes at his friends every time you make a shot.

It's hard to be an ambler if you're a woman. An ambling woman isn't a Power Image, if you know what I mean; you're supposed to walk briskly all the time, like That Girl on her way to an audition, even if you're only on your way to pick up the kids from daycare. It's also kind of hard to be a gambler if you're a woman; even if you dress like Sharon Stone in *Casino* — belted pantsuit, colourful scarf, beehive, big earrings and platform shoes — nobody in Toronto will take you seriously. In fact, that kind of outfit can really work against you as you go to place your quarter on the edge of the pool table.

The only thing I've been accused of gambling with recently is my life — mostly by my parents, who want me to get a "real" job and buy RRSPs, and also by anti-smoking lobbyists like Mendelson Joe, who have told me they would like me a whole lot better if I would just quit smoking.

I've only won at gambling twice in my life, and both times I was with the same person — code name: the Angie-Christ. This old friend has since become my sort of human version of a Lucky Troll. If I don't take her with me, I just don't win.

A couple of years ago, she talked me into going to the Woodbine racetrack, and I placed a $2 bet, my first ever, on Mark Harmon IV, a horse with a to-scoff-at track record. Two minutes later, Angie and I were flying out of that place, which was packed to the rafters with what she described as "murderers and criminals" — a catch-all way of describing the vibe of complete desperation that permeated the place like Elisabeth Shue's perfume in *Leaving Las Vegas* — with 120 big fat dollars bulging out of my wallet and a kind of weird, guilty thrill thrumming through my body. I was afraid to stay — afraid I might get hooked.

Recently, Angie talked me into playing bingo with her at Bingo Country, a subterranean bingo palace beneath a No Frills grocery store in Parkdale. Standing outside the door were a couple of heavy-looking types — long hair, leather vests with no shirts, tattooed hairy arms — looking like they were ready to roll the first little old lady who hobbled up the steps with a $2,000 jackpot in her purse.

We were a bit late, so we went to a side counter, and Angie just yelled, "Give us everything!" Eight bucks later I was sitting at one of the many tables, frantically searching through a sheaf of multicoloured papers, visions of my old office-temping days dancing through my head as I filed and sorted them according to some sort of mysterious bingo lingo. Four Corners: $50. Double Line: $100. The H: $200. Full Card: $1,000. Wow! I would have to phone thirty magazines, make seventeen pitches to each, wait three months for them to get back to me, wait another three months for my story to get published, and finally wait another three months for the cheque to make $1,000 in real life.

A mild-mannered man smoking a cigarette got up behind an electronic pulpit and began to read the number off the first ball, which was shown on several TV sets around the room. At this point I was hysterical. I didn't have the right card. I couldn't get the top off my bingo dabber. There was only one thing to do: light a cigarette and smoke it while Angie patiently put my affairs in order, miraculously marking her card at the same time.

Shaking, I caught up with the bingo caller, dabbing the first three numbers and the Free Space. Then the next number was called, and the next, and I found myself shooting straight out of my seat, like the know-it-all kid in grade school who can't wait to tell the teacher the answer, yelling "Bingo!"

Pasty, chain-smoking faces looked at me dubiously. The red-haired lady surrounded by a Noah's ark's worth of ceramic animals; the two heroin addicts babysitting the same card at the end of the table; the overweight man with a week's worth of sandwiches wrapped in plastic before him; the teenage girls with twenty cards each and single potato chips poised between their long, pierced nails; the old lady wearing a plastic bonnet with curlers peeking out — they all stared at me, breathing cyanide and nicotine from their nostrils, as if they all knew that I had made some terrible clerical error, some horrible social gaffe, mistaken a 6 for a 9 or just called "Bingo!" for the hell of it, or that I just wanted to win so very badly that I had a case of premature "Bingo".

A nice lady in an apron came over and checked my card, and

then, as I was exclaiming, "It's my first time! I won at playing bingo my very first time and with the first five numbers!", I heard the bingo caller over the loudspeaker, talking about somebody who was going to be "our Bingo Queen for tonight." And then $25 was brought to me in a mug. I sat there for the rest of the evening, beaming and thinking, "I am the Bingo Queen. Yes, I am. I'm special. I won."

Soon I was dabbing away at several cards at once, just like the most jaded of bingo players, swilling Coca-Cola as if it were the nectar of the gods, lighting cigarettes and waving the smoke over the cards like a shaman. Our hearts racing and our minds aflutter, not from the thrill of winning but from the amount of cigarette smoke in the place, Angie and I left the bingo palace exhausted, a new savoir faire — no make that *amble* — in our walk. Of course, we didn't amble too much, lest we get rolled for my $25 by those guys at the door. I might be ambling and gambling, but midnight rambling, especially in Parkdale, is still not a good idea for chicks.

# Food For The Soul

Sometimes a meal is more than a good meal. Sometimes it is a gastronomic process that shows us the way to transformation and enlightenment.

A good meal, when prepared and presented correctly, allows cultural, social and sexual revolutions to take place in between courses. It reinforces your gut feelings, awakens long slumbering instincts and allows your own third chakra to, like the Buddha's, light up the room with divine radiation. It restores the power of speech to the mute, causes normally dignified ladies to grunt and groan with pleasure, renews fertility and bestows hope, inspiration and creativity on the spiritually bereft.

I had such a meal Friday night at The Universal Grill at Shaw and Dupont, where cultural guru Byron Ayanoglu was celebrating the release of his new cookbook, *Mediterranean Cooking*, which he co-authored with his lover, Algis Kemezys. Byron, a writer and food critic living in Montreal, makes no secret of food's relationship to art, love and life. He treated me to a taste of his ideal meal — a Utopian feast fit for a bodacious Baudelaire — which slyly nurtured the outrageous wounds suffered by my wailing inner Julia Child.

First, we were treated to relaxing after-work Martinis served in chilled glasses, at the bottom of which were live goldfish sparkling like coins. The trained goldfish leapt willingly into our mouths, tickled our glottises and slid into our stomachs, where they were dive-bombed by explosive pearls of caviar ferried into our mouths on silky slivers of avocado. I guess the wriggling and wiggling goldfish tickling our solar plexuses got to us, because before we knew it, all the guests flung off their sequined jackets and began doing the frug while the D.J. played "The Happening" and projected colorful, amoebic oil and water images on the wall.

After dancing The King Tut with Byron — which, like Batman, requires you to make V's with your fingers and slide them past your eyes — Byron invited us all to sit down at the table and cleanse our palates with a sorbet made from the collected frozen tears of all the Little Old Ladies in the world who had wept miserably at the death of Princess Diana. As we ate, our own tears slid slowly down our cheeks, and we joined hands and asked for the Infinite Presence to grace us with Divine Compassion.

Then the waiters, who were dressed as eunuchs in togas of flowing chiffon, sang an original aria as they brought us each a bowl of Bull Bouillon — a clear, warm broth distilled from the hearts and testicles of the Champion Running Bulls in Spain. This glorious liquid gave us strength and a renewed sense of political awareness, and a spirited argument soon broke out among the guests, whose lips bled red as they suckled from a bottle of fine wine as old as The Whore of Babylon. Then the waiters brought out the next course, a salad of shredded red Love Apples and rare wild flowers found growing around Jim Morisson's grave in Paris. Before we knew it, high-heeled shoes were slipped off stocking feet and hands began wandering beneath the table, leading to squeaks and squeals of unexpected delight.

Our faces and bosoms flushed, we then found ourselves ready for the fish course, which was hauled in on a stretcher and placed on the table. Byron slit open the fish's glittering belly, only to reveal another fish inside, and then another fish, and another fish, and so on, until finally, inside the smallest fish we found the diamond ring I lost down the sink drain many years ago. As we pondered the miracle of this and the upcoming transformation of the Piscean Age into the Aquarian age, the waiter served us a side dish in which anthropods with Jurassic-era DNA were suspended in quivering amber blocks of aspic. As we consumed this delicacy, we found ourselves growing very wise and connected at the birthplace of the collective unconscious. We exchanged knowing looks rather than words, as the aspic had granted us telepathic powers.

The fish course was followed by a bowl of cold, bright red beet soup slashed with sour cream. When I asked Byron what this was called, he replied, "Revenge — for it is a dish best served cold." As we ate it, murderous feelings of insecurity and resentment permeated our beings; the soup ran down our chins like blood as we reflected bitterly on mankind's darker aspects — cruelty, cannibilism, genocide. This was followed by the Grand Presentation of the Mighty Roast Beast: a charred pink animal resting in a pool of its own juice. We tore the beast to pieces, first with a chain saw and then — after that short-circuited — with our claws. After this ritual re-enactment of primitive bestial consumption was over, we were served another sorbet, this one made of morning dew collected from the grass around Stonehenge on the morning of the Summer Solstice. Stars of hope again shone in everyone's eyes, like the headlights of landing U.F.O.s.

The meal concluded with espresso and a selection of petit fours constructed from layers of pastry patterned after the lacy petticoats of suffragettes; a caramelized pudding made from the Milk of Kindness, squeezed from the udders of a unicorn; and towering, bejewelled vases of Jello 1-2-3.

After savouring hours of witty repartee and the mysterious flavour of a rare Brandy — rescued from an ancient pirate ship recently discovered at the Bottom of The Bermuda Triangle — we went home, convinced that somehow, between the soup and the dessert, the Universe had changed for the betterment of all mankind.

# The Anti-Martha Stewart Cometh!

Some have said that I have a dark side. Perhaps that's how I came to be fascinated by Black Jell-O.

There is something about Black Jell-O that draws you deep into its mysterious depths and causes you to lose the only thing you really own in life: yourself. Heed this sorry tale, dear reader, and consider yourself forewarned about this gelatinous berry-flavoured dessert, lest you, too, do something you will forever regret.

It was the day before Siobhan's fortieth birthday. Our friend Fleur, who also had a birthday that week, called up Kitten and hissed in that way that means "Don't screw this one up": "I'm throwing a party tomorrow. It will be up to you and Donna to provide a cake."

Kitten, who is the Nurturing Single Friend of my world, called me up and said, "Meet me in fifteen minutes at the Dominion, babe. In the cake aisle."

"In the cake aisle," I replied and hung up. This was an important mission. Not only was this Siobhan's big Four-O, but Kitten and I have a history when it comes to making cakes.

I once made a cake out of plaster. It was 7 feet tall and 7 feet across on the bottom layer. It was an architectural wonder decorated with gargoyles and flowers made out of real cookie dough. The dough was painted gold and bugs crawled in and out of the centre of the blossoms. Black-and-white photographs of my heroin-addicted-looking friends were pressed into the sides of the cake, and at the top a model airplane was caught crashing into the wedding of two skeletons dressed as a bride and groom. I was very proud of it.

It sat on the front lawn of Garnet Press for exactly two weeks in

1986, until vandals came along and trashed it. Before this happened, Kitten used to call me up and say, "Meet me in fifteen minutes at Garnet Press. By the cake."

"By the cake," I would reply and hang up. Who knew then that I would offend once more by creating another monstrous, horrible dessert.

I found Kitten lurking in the cake aisle. "Chocolate, chocolate fudge, confetti, butter pecan, carrot cake," she was muttering, like Glenn Gould before a set of as-yet-unplayed piano keys.

"Sparklers, marshmallows, musical candles, jujubes, whipped cream," I muttered back with the grouchy, driven focus of architect Howard Roark in *The Fountainhead*. Suddenly, my eyes lit on an in-store display that drove two words into my subconscious: Black Jell-O.

Black Jell-O. Black JELL-O. BLACK JELL-O!

I had a flash. We would not bake any old boring old cake! We would create something using Black Jell-O that nobody in this universe had ever seen before. We would create an *objet d'art*, a nod to postmodern malaise and yes, even a fashion statement! You see, we would take white marshmallows, snip them into petal shapes and create daisies. We would use those little candies from the seventies, the ones that have sayings on them like "I Love You" and "Be Mine", for the centre of each flower. And then we would line a mould with the candy-marshmellow daisies and fill it with Black Jell-O. When the Jell-O was unmoulded, the white marshmallows against the Jet-Black Jell-O would look like flowers set in Lucite. We'd decorate it with whipped cream, stick sparklers in it...and it would look really cool and be practically fat-free.

You have to understand that at the time I was not myself. It was the Anti-Martha Stewart in me talking, and Kitten got caught up in my charismatic fervour. Kitten and I purchased the necessary materials to pursue our vision and went to her apartment. Roughly two hours later, we had managed, with hands white as a mime's, to line the bowl with daisies. But the minute we poured the hot, inky Black Jell-O into the bowl, the petals floated to the surface like leaves on a pond.

We had to start again. Having concluded that cooking actually *is* rocket science, Kitten decided that the solution to our daisy dilemma was to pour the Black Jell-O, slightly gelled, into the mould throughout the evening, so that our presentation would be ready for the next morning. At this point, she decided to go out and meet Siobhan, the birthday girl, for a drink. I thought this a bit strange, as Kitten rarely drinks. I went home to rest up for the big party.

The next morning I woke up and called Kitten. "How's the Jell-O?" I cheerily inquired.

A long silence. "I put it in the microwave."

The Anti-Martha Stewart in me howled.

Apparently, after drinking two litres of red wine at one of those faux English pubs, Kitten came home, opened the fridge, didn't like the way the Black Jell-O looked all bumpy and grainy, and put it in the microwave to give it that smooth, glassy sheen we were after. The result was complete artistic ruin.

Furthermore, Kitten was feeling so bad from her overindulgence the night before that she could not even lift her head from the pillow. Therefore, it became my responsibility to go and buy a new cake.

Unfortunately, the only cakes they had left at the Loblaws bakery were for children. I chose a nice, rainbow-coloured cake with a hungover-looking clown lying on top of it and asked the clerk to write, "Happy Birthday, Babes," on the top. However, in the cab I lifted the lid of the cake box to take a peek and noticed that she had written "Happy Birthday, Babies."

It really looked like I had put a lot of thought into this.

I went to the party, embarrassing Last-Minute Children's Birthday Cake in hand, babbling about microwaves and daisies and postmodern malaise. Meanwhile, the Anti-Martha Stewart in me smiled evilly somewhere in the Black Jell-O of my mind.

# The Virtues of Messiness

My parents called the other day, and they're coming to town. Uh-oh. This is news that always strikes an ominous chord in my heart — not because they are particularly oppressive, eccentric or scary; I'm the oppressive, eccentric and scary one in the family. The fact that my parents are coming to town fills my soul with dread because it means I will finally have to do something I have successfully avoided doing for the past six months — no, make that the last thirty-five years. I will have to (gulp)…CLEAN UP MY ROOM!

If you are a friend of mine and have ever seen my room or rooms, you will immediately identify with the enormity of this task. I am a Neat Freak's living nightmare.

Just my rotten luck, most of my friends happen to be neat freaks who own living rooms that look like sets from *Melrose Place*. They can't sleep at night knowing that there are seven or eight filthy old mugs with science projects growing in them lined up next to my computer. They know about the potato-chip crumbs in my bed, the overflowing ashtrays, the heaps of clothing that obstruct every surface, the toothpaste tube with the lost top, the extra cardboard toilet paper tubes I collect, plus the eight million little scraps of paper that decorate my place like leaves on a tree. From their point of view, I am definitely missing a few screws, as well as a few mops, sponges and pails.

"Why don't you get organized?" is the question I have been asked most frequently in my life by well-meaning acquaintances who look at me with a mixture of disgust and pity. I happen to think I am very well organized. I don't need their pity. All is well in my earthly domain. I'm happy! I have a pet dust-bunny named Happy living under my bed…

I read once, in one of the many New Age self-help books that are piled up next to the sink where dishes and foodstuffs should be, that there are two kinds of people in this world: people who are organized without but a mess within, and people who are disorganized without but have organized souls. I think I fall into the latter category. I have often thought to myself, "How can someone who owns so many old Martha Stewart magazines and books on Feng Shui be so messy? Isn't your home, which is an extension of your body, also the temple of your soul?" If that's the case, I live in an archeological ruin, full of valuable, biodegradable old newspapers, beneath which are buried the secrets to existence.

My messiness is evidence that I have my priorities straight. I'm a writer, not an interior decorator. People who suggest that I acquire an expensive filing system for all my papers don't realize that I already have a fully functional system. The entire top of my desk is a giant In Tray. The floor serves as the Out Tray. When the mountain of papers, computer disks, flyers and press releases reaches a certain height, things just naturally fall to the floor, by which time I am probably done with the project and can throw it all out. Anything that stays on the desk, I keep. Anything on the floor, I throw out. I don't have to waste two brain cells thinking about it.

I am the first to admit that my slothfulness has become legendary. For that reason, I have outlawed flash photography in my place. Once, to torture me, my old landlord Herb Tookey took a picture of my room at the Cameron Hotel and threatened to send it to *Frank* magazine unless I cleaned up. This past December, I arrived home to find that my apartment had been replaced by an identical, much cleaner version of itself. There was an apologetic note from my good friend Fleur that read, "I just couldn't help myself."

My own mother, who is a well-known artist in the Kingston-Ottawa area, has been so traumatized by my lifestyle — or lack of it — that she has done an incredibly detailed series of paintings called *Donna's Room*, which have sold quite well. I guess these works of art are popular because everybody has a slob like me in their life. If you look closely, you will see that she has included every true-to-life stray sock, water ring on the desk and crumpled piece of paper on the floor. The only thing missing is the pantyhose hanging from the chandelier (which, unrealistically, actually has a working lightbulb in it in the painting).

I have also read that being messy is a subconscious way for an adult to rebel against authority. Perhaps there is something deep inside of me that truly believes that if I don't make my bed, Mike Harris will renege on his political decision to punish the poor. Personally, I think it's some kind of self-destructive writer personality trait thing.

But I have to draw a line in the dust somewhere. If you'll excuse me, I have to go and clean up my room. I don't want to make my mother cry…or give her any more ideas for her art.

# True Ghost Stories

My first experience with a real ghost was at my grandfather's small cabin in Tisdale, Saskatchewan, in 1965. My little sister and I slept toe-to-toe on the couch in the living room. Every night, from about two till five, I would lie wide awake, fraught with terror, listening to what sounded like some mysterious entity throwing pots and pans and hunks of lumber around in the kitchen while my sister snored away, blissfully oblivious to the performance in the next room. It sounded like Buddy Rich practising in there.

The next morning, over a bowl of Weetabix, I would politely inquire of my grandparents about the noises in the kitchen. They would exchange significant looks, smile and jovially inform me that it was "just the ghost."

Just the ghost. That's like saying it was "just the plague". Was the world that I was about to grow up in so terrible that grown-ups were expected to take a horrible, scary thing like a ghost for granted and even joke about it as if they were renting the place to unsuspecting tenants? The answer is yes.

My next major encounter with a restless spirit (actually, the place was more like a mosh pit of restless spirits) was in Toronto in 1981. Two other people and I rented a house at 644 Richmond Street West. Before long, those two people moved out, citing really mature, grown-up reasons for breaking their lease like, "This place is haunted! I'm outta here!" and "I want to live in a place where I'm not afraid to go down the dark hallway to the bathroom at night." During my four-month attempt to rent this place, I went through a total of eleven roommates — all of whom tried to leave in the middle of the night without telling me because they "just had to get out of there."

You can make fun of me if you want, I don't care. Every time I think about it I still get scared.

My first clue that something might be wrong with the house, which looks just like any other urban attached home, was the number of wild cats that clustered around the place. There were hundreds of cats living in the shed in the backyard, most of them black with big round eyes that watched your every move.

My second clue was that I was afraid to go into the basement. I lived for four months in that house and did not go down there once. It was as though the house knew that I was afraid of what was in its bowels, and many times when I was studying in the living room I would hear a creak, and then the basement door — which I had latched shut just minutes before — would open very slowly, as if it were taunting me, daring me to go downstairs. I would shut the door again, latch it, and then minutes later it would be standing wide open again.

The antics of the basement door were nothing compared to the nightly pyrotechnics in the bedroom at the top of the stairs. My roommate Kareen and I would sit on her bed and watch what looked like a brilliant little blue ball of electricity snake out of her closet and crackle up the side of her wicker shelving unit. Then her clothes began to fall one by one from their hangers, as if being pulled off by an invisible hand. Another time, Kareen and my friend Bob the Photographer were sitting in the living room, joking about "the ghost," when an empty, newly washed ashtray on the coffee table split exactly in half, and the two halves sped off either side of the coffee table and smashed to the floor. Ghosts don't have a sense of humour.

Being a second-year film student at York University, I thought the logical thing to do would be to try and capture some of this weird stuff on film. I booked a total of eight Super-8 cameras from York, but every time I tried to shoot film in the house, the batteries — no matter how new they were — went completely dead. It was as if something was sucking up and living off the energy in the batteries. One day, after putting four different brand-new batteries from four different stores into two different cameras and realizing I could not get that needle in the window of either camera out of the dead red zone, I just sat at the top of the stairs, surrounded by empty battery package wrappings, and cried.

Then some really heavy, bizarre stuff began to happen. Hand prints would emerge from the wall in the downstairs hallway, no matter how many times my roommates or I painted the wall over. And I came home one day to find my antique dresser shoved to the other end of the room.

This was complemented by minor annoying activity. I was finding chess pieces in really weird places: a pawn in a cutlery drawer, a white knight sitting halfway up the stairs. One night we were all woken up by a smell like gasoline. We were greeted in the living room by the sight of the chandelier spinning — not swaying gently or teetering, but actually *spinning* in its socket like a motorized mirror ball.

Disturbed but ever the skeptic, I soon found myself living in the house alone. I was trapped in a lease and, being a poor student, I didn't have the resources to get out. I ignored the mysterious pounding on and rattling of the bathroom door each time I took a shower; the tall, black ominous figure that I thought I saw lurking at the door of my bedroom every night; and the fact that the face of my alarm clock, instead of hands, was now rotating.

I lived there for another week, until one night I came home, opened my front door and saw a shaft of bright blue light, with no source I could see, illuminating the bottom of the stairs with a halogen-like brilliance. Then from upstairs I heard a familiar sound — the sound of something throwing lumber, cutlery, plates and pots and pans around. Terrified, I ran to a phone and arranged to move in with my boyfriend in Cabbagetown that night.

As time goes by, I've heard more about that house — how the number 644 is a malefic number in Chinese numerology, and how one ex-roommate looked up the history of the building in the city archives and found out that, yes, a murder had taken place there at the base of the stairs.

On the other hand, friends of mine — Runt, the famous mural painter, and Colin Brunton, the equally famous film producer (*Roadkill, Highway 61*) — moved into that house after me, fixed it up and seemed to have no problem at all. I could only deduce that the evil spirits in that house were afraid of Colin and Runt. I mean, Runt, in 1982, with a couple of beers in him and a paintbrush in hand, could be pretty scary.

I decided to chalk up my experience to some kind of stress-induced hysteria until one day, years later, Colin mentioned quite casually that no matter how many times they sanded the wall and painted it over, they couldn't quite get these hand prints in the hallway to disappear...

Relax, I tell myself now. After all, it was "just a ghost".

# Things That Go Bump in the Night

THUMP! THWACK! CREAK...CREAAAAK! THWUMP! THWUMP! THWUMP! WHACK! CREAK...CREAAAAK!

It is 3:30 in the morning. What in God's name are they doing up there? It sounds like the timbers of the *Titanic* breaking up before she finally sinks to her final resting place beneath the sea. THUMP...THUMP...THUMP...THUMP...WHACK! What the hell is going on? This is no time to rearrange the furniture. It is 3:30 in the morning! THUMP, THUMP, CRASH! THUMP, THUMP, CRASH!

They can't possibly be having sex...who has sex like that?

THUMP. (Silence.) THUMP! (Long silence.) THUMP, THUMP, THUMP, THUMPITY, THUMPITY, THUMPITY,

THUMPITY. (Long silence.) THUMPITY, THUMPITY, THUMPITY, THUMPITY. CRASH! BANG! OOF! POW! BAM!

What the hell? Have they got Batman and Robin up there?

I sit up in bed and glare at the ceiling. Silence. More silence. Good. Silence. Silence again. Aaaah! They've finally spent themselves. Thank God.

Then slowly, subtly, softly, it begins again with one long "creeeeaaaaak", like a door opening by itself in a haunted house. Then another one and another one until all I'm hearing is CREAK, SQUEAK, CREAK, SQUEAK, THUMP, SQUEEEEAAAAK! And then THUMP! THUMP! THUMP!

My God, this is awful. It sounds like they're beating mice to death with mallets. It sounds like they're bowling with frozen turkeys and using Coke bottles for pins. It sounds like they're dismembering an oak tree with an old rusty saw and then throwing the pieces around for fun.

"Hey! Knock it off!" I yell, but my voice is lost against the persistent THUMP, THUMP, THUMP against the walls.

5:30 a.m. It's been two hours and they're still at it. I am still staring at the ceiling. I hope it holds. No — I HOPE THEY FALL THROUGH THE CEILING. That would show them! I hope they fall right into my bed so I can give them a piece of my mind. God, I've got a big meeting tomorrow. I don't think I'm going to make it. My eyes are wide and rheumy — I can feel the bags starting to form under them.

THUMP. THUMP. THUMP. THUMP. WHACK. BANG. CRASH. CREAK.

Just what the hell are they doing up there?

It sounds like he's got her tied up in a chair, one of those big old antique leather ones with the castors, and they're rolling around on the ancient wood floors yelling, "Whoopee!" That would account for the bowling sounds. The crash I'm hearing is when the chair hits the wall.

Or he's got her tied up at one end of the room, like a goalie and he's at the other end, naked except for rollerblades, taking runs at her. The smash I'm hearing is when he, you know, scores...

THUMP! THUMP! THUMP!

Or maybe the levitating ardour of their love is actually causing the bed to do the bunny-hop, and the whole bed is travelling across the room inch by inch, like some kind of Magic Bus...

THUMP! THUMP! THUMP!

Knock. Knock. Knock.

"HEY, KNOCK IT OFF!"

Oh my God, where is that voice coming from? Wait, there's an angry rapping on my bedroom wall.

"Hello?" I say politely to the wall. It is my neighbour from next door.

"Are you going to go at it all night, bitch? Let us get some sleep. People have to work, for Christ's sake!"

"It's not *me*!" I howl plaintively. "It's the people upstairs."

"I don't care, just stop it, OK?" he yells hysterically.

"But it's driving me crazy, too!"

"Just fuck off!" yells my crazed, sleep-deprived neighbour.

This is just not fair. Here I am, suddenly single, and taking the rap for someone else's bumps in the night. I grab the broom and start banging the ceiling. THUNK, THUNK, THUNK goes the broom.

THUMP, THUMP, THUMP, they answer.

THUNK, THUNK, THUNK goes the broom.

THUMP, THUMP, THUMP.

"Jesus Christ, will you stop it? People are trying to sleep down here!" I yell to the ceiling.

THUMP. THUMP. THUMP. THUMPITY. THUMPITY. THUMPITY. CRASH. BANG.

It is like my thunking on the ceiling has only encouraged them to thump harder.

"Stop this senseless, macabre parody of the act of procreation that will only lead to heartbreak!" I scream. It is futile. It is like trying to stop the Olympics.

It's 7:20 a.m. The pounding has stopped. Sadly, I watch the dawn's light break through the window. I have had no sleep.

At 8:30 a.m., looking all cheerful and fresh, the smiling new couple descend hand in hand from their love lair, their hair still wet from the shower they shared. How can they be so chipper after all that? I guess a change really is as good as a rest.

Now 9 a.m. Outside. I wave to the neighbour next door on his way to work. He looks at me incredulously and then scurries away like I am some kind of insatiable Fuck Monster. Life really is not fair.

# Necro-Lite™

# A Day in the Life

Today I woke up at 8:15 a.m., exactly the time I told myself I would. It was nice not to be jolted awake by the alarm clock for a change. I got up, went to the kitchen and reached for a mug. There was no crud in the bottom. I put the kettle on, and while I was watching it…it actually boiled. "There goes that theory," I thought. The milk I'd bought a week before still hadn't turned sour. It was going to be a great day!

I turned on the TV. It was going to be sunny and mild — a bright blue sky scudded with a few clouds. There was no construction to report anywhere in the city. All the highways were open. The lead news item was a story about how the entire cast of *Lord of the Dance* had sprained their ankles simultaneously. Too bad. The Humane Society was pleased to report that every single homeless dog and cat had finally been adopted. And every last person at the CNE had made back the price of admission playing Crown and Anchor.

The most exciting story, however, was about how dental costs were finally going to be covered by OHIP. "It is very important that each and every citizen in Ontario wear a great big shiny smile," the government had announced.

While standing in the shower, whose steady stream of perfectly temperate water was not once interrupted by flushing toilets or running faucets elsewhere in the building, I was shocked to notice that the tattoo I had gotten in San Francisco (while under the influence of some diesel dykes I had been hanging around with) had completely disappeared. It was as if this particular batch of water had the power to rinse it away. As I stepped out of the shower, my hair dried almost instantly into the studied yet casual coiffure I prefer. Pulling my freshly washed clothes out of the laundry bag, I watched them emerge unwrinkled and professional-looking. My lips, naturally full and red, and eyes, sparkling and fringed with dark lashes, did not need makeup. Then I realized I could see perfectly without my glasses, which I joyfully threw away.

When I went to collect my mail, there were what looked like several bills from various utility and credit card companies. My heart filled with dread. Imagine my surprise when instead I found several pleasant notes from these companies thanking me for my years of patronage. However, the biggest surprise of all came when I opened a letter from Ed McMahon that read: "Congratulations, Ms. Lypchuk! You Are the Winner of 10 Million Dollars!"

Seeing as I already had $10 million — the result of a sudden windfall of uncollected royalties and residuals prompted by a change of heart on the part of certain magazines and theatres who had decided they had underpaid me for years — I was in no rush to deposit my prize. I decided to take a leisurely stroll through the park on my way to the ATM. The birds were singing and I did not step in one ounce of dog doo. The grass was green and there was not a condom or needle in sight. Happy families sporting inner tubes were on their way to one of Toronto's many unpolluted beaches. Even the rusty drinking fountain was working.

Outside the bank, a homeless man to whom I had given a quarter six years before paid me back. The ATM accepted my card on the first try. I deposited the cheque, withdrew just enough money to adopt several children, and the screen flashed, "Have a Nice Day."

On my way to the Children's Aid Society to discuss the adoptions, I ran into several friends. Each spoke enthusiastically of their work, family and friends. Each was so happy to have their health. They were not jealous, resentful, bitter or remorseful. They were looking forward to growing old, because the elderly are the most respected people in our society.

I arrived at the Children's Aid Society to find it was closed — not due to cutbacks but because all the children were being cared for. Everything, in fact, was closed. There was no need for hospitals because nobody was sick. No need for prisons or poorhouses or churches because everybody had faith in themselves.

I ducked into the phone booth and decided to check my messages. "You have 610 unheard messages," said the friendly automated voice. Then, as chains of interdigitating citizens singing

John Lennon's "Imagine" drifted past, I listened to every person I'd ever known tell me that they loved me, again and again.

Message 610 was different, however. Message 610 featured an annoyed, nasal voice: "Donna Lypchuk. It's Myra Stevens calling you from the Toronto Dominion Bank. That cheque you deposited for $10 million is a VOID sample. I'm afraid we will have to withdraw your banking privileges."

Then I woke up. It was 4:15 p.m. The alarm was screaming like a banshee. I had only meant to nap for an hour, and now my column was late. I ran a comb through my messy hair, stuck a cigarette in my mouth, stumbled to the kitchen and made myself a cup of tea. Floating on the top was a tiny, unidentified piece of crud. Sour milk? Thank God I noticed before I took the first sip.

Yes, it was going to be a great day!

# The New Anti-Joking Law

I don't mind telling you that ever since the City of Toronto passed that new Anti-Joking bylaw I've been a little depressed.

It used to be that you could joke anywhere you wanted to in Toronto — at work, in restaurants and bars, even on the subway platform. In fact, as everybody knows, the only way to make a streetcar come is to pull out a good joke. Ain't that always the way? If there's one thing I hate, it's having to throw away a perfectly good joke when the streetcar comes. Nowadays, you can't even crack a smile on the subway without somebody giving you a dirty look, just in case you might start joking.

It's hard to believe, but up until just a few years ago, people were still allowed to joke in office buildings. Then Health and Welfare Canada decided that second-hand joking was hazardous to your health. Not only were you killing yourself laughing, you were killing others too. Posters appeared, warning: "Health and Welfare Canada advises that taking in second-hand jokes is hazardous to your health." They featured a grim-looking photograph of a man who had "died laughing". The CBC even got in on the act, producing less and less entertaining programming in an effort to persuade people to stop thinking that joking was cool.

This had the opposite effect on the nation's youth, who began to see joking as a glamorous, taboo way of rebelling against authority. Teenagers who didn't normally have a sense of humour were soon seen tickling each other in the joking area of their high school.

Canadian writers, performers and entertainers fled to the United States in droves so that they could joke all they wanted — and even get paid for it. Meanwhile in Canada, businesses and agencies reacted to pressure from fanatical No Joking groups by cloistering jokers in small, unventilated rooms during their fifteen-minute breaks.

Some desperate jokers resorted to sneaking a small pun in the company washroom, or eventually ended up joking outside their buildings. To add to the woes of heavy jokers, the government slapped a tax on jokes, hoping that the extra expense would eventually save lives. This scheme backfired, and the law only served to create a thriving black market that sold cheap American jokes to Canadians.

Perhaps fed up with having to go outside to scream a simple ten-minute joke above the annoying howl of the bitterly cold Canadian wind, many jokers joined the ranks of the non-jokers. However many realized that, as with heroin or cocaine, they were hopelessly addicted to joking and had to resign themselves to a higher power (no, not God, but one of those world-renowned pharmaceutical companies) to get over their addiction.

One of the most popular devices was an Anti-Joking patch, which, when applied to the jokers' forearms, released timed dosages of a substance that produced the same kind of endorphins as those found in a joker's brain when he was experiencing, for example, an episode of *Seeing Things*. This way the joker was gently weaned off all humour, until he no longer longed for satire or blond jokes, and was instead dutifully productive and wept quietly at his desk like all of the other non-jokers. This person was also persuaded to invest the money that he otherwise wasted while telling or listening to jokes in a special little treat for himself, like a mutual fund.

But now that the City of Toronto has passed a law that prohibits joking in bars and restaurants, it is virtually impossible to have a good time. Even though it seems that some of our citizens have been able to beat the system by enjoying a private joke amongst themselves (as long as the proprietor of the establishment has warned them about the law before they start up), the City of Toronto has struck the fear of God in us all by slapping a $5,000 fine on a restaurant owner who allowed a couple of clowns to yuk it up in his tiny, four-table restaurant. Quite unfairly, the same law-keepers ignored the brazen, full-blown comedy revue that was breaking out spontaneously in the bar down the street.

I know joking can be bad for you and that there are some places where joking doesn't belong — in church or the mortuary — but the situation here in the City of Toronto is getting far too serious. If we don't watch it, Toronto is going to get a reputation as a cold, humourless town, and nobody will come here to shoot American comedies any more.

I'll admit it. I'm addicted. Like most people, I started joking when I was sixteen, and now I find it hard to stop. I can appreciate the fact that non-jokers have as many rights as jokers, but I wish the City of Toronto would lighten up and let me laugh again. Let's face it, nothing goes better with a cold, frosty glass of Canadian beer, after a long, hard day at work, than a couple of stale jokes. And maybe a cigarette.

# Elderly Abuse

It's about time that someone finally addressed the slightly taboo subject of elderly abuse. Quite frankly, I think the situation is out of control!

Oh sure, there's the odd senior citizen (and most of them really are quite odd, don't you think?) who's a genuine victim of our perverse, greedy, soul-sucking society. They end up locked in government-subsidized homes, drugged out of their minds and unable to stop their ungrateful children from spending their hard-earned nest eggs on frivolities like extra-quiet dishwashers, shares of Bre-X and Tickle Me Elmo dolls. However, those examples are few and far between, although subject to vast coverage by the media, who, if you ask me, have been making a rule out of the exception.

And just who do you think is responsible for writing these horror stories, which often feature photographs of senior citizens tied to their beds, eating dog food in cafeterias, or on their knees, forced to work as sex slaves in the local biker hangout? Journalists who are approaching retirement, that's who! Baby Boomers in whose best interest it is to portray Canada's aging population in the most pathetic light possible, so that we will continue to pour hundreds of thousands of dollars of our hard-earned money into the Canada Pension Plan — which of course will not be there for us come 2010, when our eyesight, hearing and hip joints finally give out.

We have been tricked this way before by the Baby Boomers, who have always promised us jobs like they've had, houses like they've had and a virtually Utopian society full of wonderful things such as hair implants, breast augmentation and cottage retreats. The Baby Boomers, who promised us a world of unlimited renewable resources, have instead left us to float aimlessly in the gases left over from their greedy belches — the result of living full, prosperous lives in which they permitted themselves to "consume" the world with a passion. There is nothing left for us. Such a blatant disregard for our future and what we would have to contend with as a result of their irresponsible, even capricious actions, can be described as a massive case of collective child abuse.

If you ask me, the elderly in our society have it really easy, sitting around watching TV all day and getting their three squares; one would think that they were lucky enough to be prison inmates. People like to write and talk about abuse of "the elderly", but nobody writes or talks about the way the elderly abuse *us*. Abuse by the elderly is rampant, and something must be done about it!

For instance, have you ever noticed how most so-called disabled seniors turn into Ninja warriors at the first indication they may not get their way? You see this every day at the TTC stop, as the elderly whip and wield their canes about innocent people's ankles in the quest to be the first to board the bus. Of course, nobody ever says anything about this rude behaviour, such as, "Ow, little old lady, I'll never dance again," because we have this inherent respect for people who are allegedly facing an imminent natural demise.

However, we don't treat people who are about to die unnaturally in our society with the same respect: we shove the young man with full-blown Kaposi's sarcoma to the back of the line; tell the young, Type-A executive with the heart condition to work until midnight every day or lose his job; and we ignore those frantic calls to the Children's Aid Society about the infant starving to death next door. My point is, we are all dying a little bit every day, so there is no reason to show those who are more youthful than you such disrespect.

Most senior citizens will lead you to believe that they are helpless as newborn gerbils, forcing you to read to them, do their dishes and make their beds, when in reality they are possessed of an almost supernatural excess of energy. Like vampires, most old people are nocturnal creatures who are capable of staying up all night. Anyone who has ever gone on a holiday with a senior citizen will attest to their preternatural strength as they lead you on a tour of Disneyland, Busch Gardens, Cape Canaveral, shopping, sightseeing on the bus and then on to the lobster restaurant to enjoy some Don Ho-inspired kabuki. They will cruelly ignore your pleas for mercy, knowing full well that your tender young body requires food and at least seven hours of sleep to function.

However, the height of elderly abuse is what I call the deliberate withholding of wisdom. Contrary to the image of the benign old bubbie or the gentle grandfather put forth to us in story and song, most old people really get a kick out of watching us "make our own mistakes". It is as if they are relishing that moment when we can come to them, complaining of our woes, so that they can say, "I told you so," even though they never did. Whenever you ask an old person, "Why did you let me do that when you knew it would just fuck up?", they almost always smile like angels and, rather sadistically, reply: "It's important for you to make your own mistakes."

Letting us make our own mistakes is the most expedient and convenient way for the elderly to get even with us for patronizing them with our low expectations all of these years. It's time we woke up and realized that far from being senile, helpless and delicate, most of those smart, wily, super-energized old people can really kick ass.

# Sports We'd Like to See

Here comes a really sexist comment: the only reason I watch sports is because I like the way shiny white Lycra pants, shrink-wrapped over nicely toned male buttocks, stand out so starkly against vivid green Astroturf.

There. I'm glad that's out of the way. Otherwise, I must confess I have no real interest in sports — I just turn on the TV and admire the screen the way one might admire a bright yet confusing surrealist painting in the AGO.

Obviously, I am not part of the general bulk of the population, which apparently has a passion for being full-time onlookers. If I experience a victory, I want it to be mine. I want some ParticipAction! Sports should be hard work. There should be blood, sweat, tears and a gigantic sum of money (or a nicely-toned man wearing Lycra pants, if no money is available) awarded to you at the end. The loser should be sentenced to hard labour or maybe even death.

After all, isn't sports really a dress rehearsal for life? Who wants to spend their life being some kind of voyeur, always wryly commenting on the action after the fact? Here are some recently invented *useful* sports that will not only give you a thrill, but will help you brush up on your survival skills as well:

## CD Discus Throwing:

The idea is to get rid of your reject CDs and decapitate any onlookers on the sidelines. Grab that Peter Frampton live re-release, that soundtrack to *The Way We Were* and that *Fabulous Hits of the '50s* compilation and hurl them at your opponent. The person who gets rid of their used CDs without suffering a cut to their face wins. The loser must collect all the bad disks and make their friends listen to them. This is a handy way to get rid of the rejects in your CD tower. However, if you throw a CD in the air and it comes back to you, it was really yours all along.

## Vacuum Bumper Cars:

Here is a sport you can play right on your living-room carpet. There are usually two teams. The Fantom Furies vs. the Dirt Devils, for instance. Each team consists of six housewives wearing ankle-length evening gowns. The idea is to use the powerful suction of your upright vacuum cleaner to catch the hems on the dresses of the opposing team. The team that manages to completely strip the other team wins. This can be a very exciting game because high-speed vacuum cleaners tend to choke and burst into flames when vacuuming up items like the hems of evening gowns.

## Black Lycra Turtleneck Wrestling:

This dangerous sport is not for the faint of heart or lengthy of limb. There is only one contestant in this game — you. The idea is to put the black turtleneck on and then try to take it off without falling to the floor or being strangled. Adventurous types can try a turtleneck one size too small.

## The Terrible Twos:

This is a gruelling test of an individual's endurance and skill. Basically, a Barney puppet or *Star Wars* artifact is placed in a net. The goalie wears shin guards and a face mask while being pummelled by a team of shrieking two-year-olds, whose object is to get the toy. The game is over when everybody has had a good cry and has been settled down for a nap.

## Stiletto Heel Balance Beam:

This is a sport I dare any professional athlete to play. First, put on a pair of this season's new killer heels — stilettos by Manolo Blahnik or even le château will do. Throw your shoulders back, suck in your stomach and hold your chin up. Now try to walk. If you can do it, you win! Advanced level: take a stroll on a golf course.

### Film Festival Press-Pass Triathlon:

Race over to the host hotel on your bike and up three flights to the Press Office. Be informed of important documents missing. Race back down three flights of stairs. Bicycle back home to obtain important missing documents. Bicycle back. Race back up three flights. Present documents. Be sent to end of line. March in place while waiting. Use elbows to nudge away competition. Obtain Press Pass. Proceed to nearest party. Drink copious amounts of alcohol. Dance with obscure German documentary filmmaker. Do push-ups with obscure German documentary filmmaker till dawn. Bicycle back home. Drink copious amounts of Gatorade. Collapse in bed. If you wake up the next day and can still move your head without everything looking like an endless dizzying pan from a DePalma movie, you win!

# The Twelve Despicable Days of Christmas

### Day one:

Only twelve shopping days left until Christmas. Big deal. I've got plenty of time. Think I'll lie down, watch more *Seinfeld* and...[*snore*]

### Day two:

Only eleven shopping days left until Christmas. I'd better get serious. Wonder how late the Eaton Centre is open...feeling sleepy again...[*snore*]

Day three:

Took a walk around the neighbourhood, and the Halloween decorations are down. This is a definite omen. Today, after work, I will make an effort to get my Christmas shopping done.

Day four:

Forgot I had to go to the office Christmas party last night, so I didn't go shopping after work. Ow. What's that horrible sound? Oh, it's only the unbearable scritch-scratching of my pen on paper...sounds like a horde of hideous rats with tiny, sharp claws scrambling around inside my brain. Must get organized. Oh look, I just found an envelope. My boss must have tucked it into my bra some time after I passed out from the eggnog. Was that before or after I photocopied my butt? I can't remember. Oh goody, it must be my Christmas bonus.

Hey, wait a minute! There's no cheque in here! It's just a card — "Happy Holidays from BrainDeath, Inc." I know they were talking about laying some people off after Christmas, but I didn't know things were this bad. Ingrates! And after all the money I made for them on the Carbon Monoxide account, even though I really don't believe in Carbon Monoxide! Well. This means I can only afford to spend about $5 on each present, or risk eviction by April. I know, I'll cross a few people off my list, like my best friend Marnie and my friend Trish, and only include the people in my life that I see just once a year: Mom, Dad, my sister, her eleven children and her husband. There! Now, I must get up, put on my clothes...the room is spinning. Really got into the eggnog last night. Think I'll lie down again, just till the room stops spinning, and then go to the Eaton Centre. Must do Christmas shopping...must not leave it until last minute...[snore]

Day five:

Had lunch with my best friend Marnie and my friend Trish today, and guess what? Marnie bought me a Rolex and Trish bought me a

$200 coffee-table book on Pre-Raphaelite art. And what was I doing? Sitting there with a big smile on my face going, "Shucks, guys, I didn't get you anything." Didn't get to do that Christmas shopping today either, because I spent so much time on hold, trying to book a train ticket home. Then I called the bus station and booked myself a $200, sixteen-hour, standing-room-only ride home that leaves at 11 p.m. Hmmm. Christmas is getting expensive.

What's that hideous noise? Sounds like a bagpipe being stabbed repeatedly with a knife. Oh, it's just Alvin and the Chipmunks singing Christmas tunes on the radio. Considering reselling book on Pre-Raphaelite art for cash to buy Christmas presents for family. Tried to sell the Rolex — it turned out to be fake.

## Day six:
Went to the Eaton Centre and bought everybody socks. That takes care of that. Even the kids could use a good pair of socks, don't you think?

## Day seven:
Spent the day gift-wrapping socks.

## Day eight:
My sister called. Turns out she got everybody socks for Christmas too. Darn. Went back to Eaton Centre and charged up millions of dollars worth of toys, board games, pen sets, fridge magnets and curling irons on credit card. As I left, Santa waved and laughed in a macabre way.

## Day nine:
Spent day in bed attempting to digest cement-like slab of fruitcake force-fed to me by well-intentioned neighbour. Smirked skeptically and scoffed bitterly while watching *It's a Wonderful Life*.

## Day ten:
Spent twenty-four hours standing on bus ride home during worst

snowstorm in decades. Accompanied by smelly, rude, drunk, singing college students and squalling babies. Threw up from bus fumes twice. Mysteriously, no fruitcake reappeared.

## Day eleven:

Spent day recovering from ingesting cement-like slab of shortbread force-fed to me by well-intentioned mother. Seven children playing Alvin and the Chipmunks incessantly. Contemplated feeding children berries from poisonous poinsettia plant. Must get out of here now, before I go stark raving mad or impale myself on the top of the tree!

## Day twelve:

Have just finished Christmas dinner. Must help Mom do dishes...Will lie down for just a minute...Am getting dirty look from sister...Should be nice to Mom, in case I lose job and have to live here...Must stay conscious to watch *How the Grinch Stole Christmas*...My new socks are so cozy...Children and Dad are unconscious now. Mom, Sis, save yourselves...Can't go on...Christmas lights getting dim...[*snore*]

# One More Pogo, Please

I enjoy being a Necrofile! I really do! The same way I love being a Breck girl. But I am contemplating journalistic celibacy from pop culture. Just because I am a Necrofile doesn't mean I have to joyously molest any old corpse that rises from the dead. *The Brady Bunch*. Herbal Essence shampoo. Studio 54. A Flock of Seagulls haircuts. *Boogie Nights*. Face glitter, lip gloss, fright wigs. Greasy old men with wide ties setting up lines of coke on their penises in the washroom...Oh, did I write that? No, I like to leave it to the mainstream media to "do" the seventies. They get off on buggering cultural stiffs like *That '70s Show*.

I go to nightclubs and it's like *Night of the Living Dead* — I keep seeing doppelgängers of horrible people that I went to high school with dancing under the disco ball. I get depressed, and the creative juices don't flow. The seventies "just don't make me dilate," as poet/singer Sahara Spracklin would say. I guess I am just not the retro individual who would have an orgasm after using Herbal Essence shampoo, like in the commercial. Hell, I don't remember getting off on the stuff the first time around.

I decided when I was seventeen that I could never trust anybody who didn't wear pointy black shoes. I look around me at the shoes people are wearing now, and all I see are round or square toes. You can tell me to Foucault off, but I look at a round shoe and I think, "This is not a shoe. This is a symbol of the complacent and regressive seventies that has returned to haunt the nineties."

The seventies were all about limitations, insecurities and vicious circles. The happy face turned sideways became Pac-Man, a vicious circle with teeth that gobbled up the goodies in life. There is no élan, no tension, no dignity, no style, no edge to the seventies, because they were all about conformity — the glitter and glam were compensating for a real spiritual void. There was a kind of smarmy flatness to life that could only be relieved by imitating *Scooby Doo*. The rounded surfaces, joyful colours, pretty lights and shag carpeting were representative of the cultural insane asylum we were in. It saddens me to see people distracting themselves with these forms of decoration again. Who can think while surrounded by such visual noise? There was nothing erotic about the costumes we sported back then, and there is nothing erotic about them now. Bring back the long, pointy, hard, sleek black shoes that everybody wore in the eighties. Resurrect New Wave.

People keep telling me we are reliving the seventies. I say, "Just what kind of seventies did *you* live through?" What is being resurrected now is everything that used to disgust and offend me. That big yellow smiley face is emblematic to me of a sick-as-shit, cookie-cutter culture that enslaves us in its complacency. In the nineties its revival is a symbol of the more concrete forms of Soma that people ingest — GHB, Ecstasy and Prozac.

I don't have memories of the seventies the way other people do. I spent my time seeking out the aesthetic antithesis of what I saw around me. I dressed in black, like that character from Chekhov, because I was "in mourning for my life." I wanted anarchy, chaos and violence. I wanted Dada, revolution and the Theatre of Blood. I wanted to feel, even if it was pain. I couldn't smile and worship the big, yellow happy face in the Church of the Pseudo-Life like everyone else. I never wore glittery shirts or went to discos. I went to the Horseshoe, the Queen City Tavern, the Edge and Larry's Hideaway. I went to see punk! Real punk rock. Hey...punk rock was part of the seventies! As Handsome Ned sang, "Where have all the punkabilly girls gone?" Hey, DJ! I'm an old punkabilly girl. Spin some records for me.

I was ruminating about all this when Colin Brunton called to remind me that the first of December is the twentieth anniversary of "The Last Pogo". The Last Pogo was a bogus event held at the Horseshoe to celebrate "the death of punk rock" in Toronto. Filmmakers Patrick Lee and Brunton managed to catch it on film, and I asked him to send the tape over. I slipped it into the player and there it was again — the Best of Toronto Punk (well, except for the Forgotten Rebels, who didn't play that night, but shoulda). For about an hour, anarchy, chaos and the Theatre of Blood reigned again as the Cardboard Brains, the Scenics, the Ugly, the Mods, the Viletones and Teenage Head lived again. Now all I ask for is one more pogo, please, before I die.

## My Fantasy Intern

The other day I was huddled around the water cooler with the staff here, discussing the Bill Clintoris/Monica Lewdinsky scandal, when suddenly one of the *eye* interns walked in and gave us one of those panicky, wide-eyed looks.

"Is this the fax machine?" he cried, putting documents in the microwave and frantically punching buttons. "The film editor wants this faxed right away!"

We watched as he blew up in a cloud of smoke. All that was visible was the battered fedora, with a placard marked "The Rookie" in the headband, that we had given him on his first day.

When the air cleared, the art director handed him a pail and told him to go to the store and fill it with microdots. "Sure!" he said, skipping off while we snickered.

The other intern was still wearing her catwoman jumpsuit from the night before, and her hair was sticking up in a big fuck-knot. "Oh wow, man," she yawned, smearing the mascara from her eyes and shoving her empty coffee cup at the editor. "Double cream, double Nutrasweet!" she barked. "I know I was supposed to be in first thing, but I had a fight with my boyfriend."

Moaning and sighing, she curled up on the sofa. "Don't mind me," she mumbled. "I'm just going catch a few winks. You guys can talk, just don't talk too loud."

"Maybe you'd like to do some photocopying for me later," suggested the production editor.

"Maybe you'd like to shove it up your ass," spat the intern. "I don't do photocopying. Do you think Courtney Love would do photocopying? I don't have to do this, you know. I'm a fucking artist. This is fucking inhuman. This coffee tastes like shit. You people are robots!" Then she stormed off.

I guess the thing we found so bewildering was just how Bill Clinton got an intern to put a cigar up her vagina for him when we can't get ours to photocopy, type, fax, file or even stop crying sometimes. I mean, we've hired hundreds over the years, and not a single one would agree to have sex with us or stick anything in any orifice. Well, except maybe that one in 1991. Hmmm...[*wavering images...dream music...*] Oh, yes, it's all coming back to me. That particular intern, what was his name?

Dirk Pike.

Dirk stood before me like a Greek god, blue eyes beaming like twin lasers, strong, firm flesh straining beneath his *eye* T-shirt.

"How can I serve you, ma'am?" he asked.

"Oh," I said, "I guess you could sit at that desk and answer the phone."

"Sure," he said, and then disappeared.

Immediately the phone rang. "That stupid intern," I thought, picking up. "He's just like all the rest. He can't even answer the phone."

"Hello?" I snapped. It was him.

"I want to fuck your head off," he whispered in a sexy voice, along with a bunch of other stuff I can't print here.

A few minutes later he showed up in my doorway, thumbs jammed in his belt loops like James Dean in *Giant*. "I'm a little bored," he said.

"Oh well," I said, "I guess you could take these photos and put them in that filing cabinet."

"Sure," he said, burying his face in my neck, ripping off my shirt, unhooking my bra with his teeth and massaging my breasts until I had an orgasm (years before Bill did it to Monica).

Then, when I asked him to fill out a form, he got on all fours and sucked my toes. Later that afternoon, when I asked him to photocopy some important papers, he flung me on the machine and took me right there while the rest of the staff carried on like nothing was happening.

This continued for weeks. Oh, occasionally the publisher would stop by my office — where the intern would be feeding me pomegranates while dressed in a polyvinyl thong, or stroking my naked body with pink strips of mink — and inquire, "Say, how's that new intern working out?"

"Oh, just fine," I would mumble from whatever manly valley my face was buried in at the time.

By the time Dirk got fired for smoking a joint on the job (it wasn't fair — he didn't inhale), I looked like Kim Basinger at the end of *9 1/2 Weeks* — you know, a drooling idiot with permanent whisker burn.

Of course, nobody at *eye* noticed. Most of them thought he was my intern*ist*, which is not surprising, given the way he always seemed to be examining my internal organs.

# Get Ready! Get Set!....WAIT!

My first drama teacher used to say, "The point of life is not to spend your time longing to be somewhere better than you are now, but to have fun trying to get there."

This is one of those comforting yet slightly disquieting platitudes designed to rationalize nearly any hardship or failure that may come your way. I find it applies to just about any situation you may encounter, except when it comes time to get ready to go to a party. Then this adage becomes, "The point of life is not to spend your time longing to be at the party, but to have fun waiting for other people to get their act together so you can call a cab and get there, because it's already after midnight and you agreed to meet people there who have probably left by now thanks to your so-called friends, goddammit!"

Getting ready to go to a party, especially if it's a big one, like a Toronto International Film Festival party or an opening at the AGO, is a big, fat ordeal that requires plenty of bedrest, the social skills of a therapist and the patience of someone who likes to grow rare orchids. There's something about going to a showy party, full of important business contacts and people dressed "just so", that dredges up the worst kind of insecurities. Beneath all the arguments, the procrastinating, the joint-smoking and fussing around with makeup that precedes one of these events is the fundamental fear that one might accidentally show up nude, the way you did in that nightmare. Or that you might suddenly find yourself lost for witty bons mots just as you are called upon to do some impromptu public speaking in front of one of those Citytv cameras that bob around town.

No wonder so many couples show up at parties acting like they've just done a living-room version of Who's Afraid of Virginia Woolf? Arguing is a way of working off pre-party tension.

People procrastinate as long they can before they go to a party, to avoid being the first to arrive. Ideally, you're supposed to behave like you were having much more fun somewhere else, at one of the bigger, more glamorous parties that you, of course, attend every night, and then decided to make room in your busy schedule at the last minute to attend this one. This is why most people never go to a party alone, or even with just their partner, but instead show up with an entourage. Arriving with a herd of nervous, well-dressed people ensures that you will not be the first to arrive or end up standing in a corner staring into your drink, alone.

Organizing an entourage can be a lot of work. As your friends' nerves will probably be chewed raw at the prospect of trying to have fun in a room filled with people who may include their ex, their current partner's ex, their former boss, that guy they want a job from, the local sociopath and the media, they will resort to anything to make sure that your route to the party will become as complicated and maze-like as possible.

These behaviours can manifest as: trying on every dress they own for three hours while you wait, just getting in the shower as you arrive to pick them up or, better yet, falling asleep in front of the TV. Of course, once you're in the cab, it's a convenient time for everyone to do all of their last-minute shopping — for cigarettes or a new pair of nylons, for example. Or a stop at the ex-boyfriend's place for a quick, pre-party altercation. Any inappropriate behaviour is fine as long as it hinders the goal of actually getting to the party.

There was a time in my life when I would not have dared to show up at a party without an entourage to support my crumbly, self-conscious writer ego. Years passed and still I insisted on stuffing drunken, drooling passengers, who had tried to anesthetize their pre-party jitters, into cabs and hauling them away with me to fancy events where they would fall onto buffet tables or urinate with great pride on the front lawn of the building. But I eventually realized that if I was going to make it to any parties at all, I would have to drop the Warhol routine and go alone.

I finally decided this after I agreed to share a taxi to a party in the East End with a very-much-in-love couple. We agreed that they would pick me up at 8, so I got all dressed up in my party duds and waited. At 8 they called and said they would be another half-hour. At 9:30 they called and said they would be picking me up by 10. At 10:30 they called and told me to expect them at 11. At midnight they finally showed up and we proceeded, not to the party, but to a bar, where they had, behind my back, agreed to meet another friend. By 1 o'clock the friend finally arrived, but I'd had a couple of glasses of wine by then and was so sleepy I went home. Who the hell feels like going to a party after five hours of waiting to go to a party? Not me.

To quote an old David Byrne song, my idea of heaven is this: "There is a party, and everyone is there / And everyone arrives at exactly the same time."

# The Hypocritic Oath

I solemnly swear that I am a hypocrite, will always be a hypocrite and will expect others to be responsible for my hypocrisy for the rest of my life. I promise to support and embellish the lies of other hypocrites and promise never to betray them or hold them responsible for their own actions.

I promise I will always feel sorry for the starving little children I see on TV, while at the same time spending $1,600 a month on Betsey Johnson dresses or Hugo Boss suits, concerts at Wonderland, a set of funky glassware pictured in *Toronto Life*, a new brass bed, sunglasses and the occasional trip to McDonald's.

I will brag at cocktail parties about what a big socialist I am at heart, yet when the fundraiser phones asking me to donate money to their cause I will pronounce in my snottiest tone: "I'm sorry, but we do not accept unsolicited telephone calls in this household," and rudely hang up.

I promise I will become a wounded healer and use my own experience, in conjunction with crystals, oils, herbs and ear candles, to heal others and better the world...at $70 a visit.

I will preach the virtues of abstinence from alcohol and drugs, yet I will happily fork out $8 to catch the latest hip drug film and hundreds of dollars to buy numerous CDs by artists devoted to popularizing and fetishizing drug culture. I will preach the virtues of drug-free living while swilling Bach herbal remedies and ODing on valerian and melatonin every night to get to sleep.

I will state to whomever will listen that I am proud to be Canadian and support our burgeoning artistic culture, yet I will fork out another $10 to see the latest Hollywood event movie and faithfully repeat the negative reviews of Canadian artistic endeavours that I read in the dailies…I will spread the word.

I solemnly promise to be a Lover of Nature. I will tend my garden as I tend my soul, watering it relentlessly with precious natural resources all summer and spraying it with pesticides until it is obvious that my morally superior soul has been blessed from above with the biggest and most beautiful garden on the street.

I will complain about cigarette smoke, yet I will drive my car every day, wear chemical-laden, designer-label perfume, work in an office with central air conditioning with screens that haven't been cleaned in years, attend a bonfire on the beach, cheer when fireworks spread their smoke across the sky on Canada Day, vote for an expansion of the Toronto airport, burn sweetgrass smudges and incense to "purify" my environment, poison the air with the fumes from my dry-cleaned clothing and fart disgusting bubbles of methane all day long.

I will weep for the plight of the cute panda bears and take my children to see them at the zoo. I will wear a little silver dolphin pin to show that I care for aquatic life, yet secretly wish that the starving, stray kitten that's been screaming at my door lately would go away and die before I have to spend my hard-earned money on a cab to the Humane Society.

I will donate money to the less fortunate, as long as they live in any other country but this one.

I will valiantly fight for the rights of women everywhere, unless of course those women are more attractive than me.

I promise to feel sorry for the homeless and avoid them on the street to kindly spare them the humiliation of asking for a quarter.

I promise to be polite and courteous and open the door for others, especially when I want them to leave.

Finally, I promise to be fair and consider all sides of every story, in case I am ever called upon to justify my own hypocrisy, which, of course, can always be explained away by the fact that everything in the universe is made up of yin and yang and the fact that opposites attract...and that appearances apparently *are* everything.

# Not Dead Yet

# New Age Tortures

I'll admit it: I'm a spiritual tramp. I have spent the past few years paying lots of money to all manner of "wellness-based" therapies, hoping they will provide me with a panacea for all my aches and pains. The only thing these alternative methods of healing seem to have cured, however, is my curiosity. I now know all I need to know about wellness-based dentistry, electromagnetic-field tracing, core-belief engineering, the Feldenkrais method, Reiki, aromatherapy, the Mozart effect and so on.

This morning I found myself trying to sum up my New Age vision quest, and all that came to mind was that Monty Python line: "No one expects the Spanish Inquisition." For the goal of New Age therapies is to get you to confess. For instance, you're lying there all blissed out, and suddenly some healer with a gentle voice sticks a needle between your front and second toe, says something about "activating the *ch'i* in your angry liver," and walks away with a sadistic chuckle while you watch your foot shudder and jerk like a dead frog in grade ten science class. Of course, the thing you immediately want to confess is: "This is silly. This isn't working. I don't feel any better. I shouldn't have come here and spent all this money," but you don't, lest the powerful Church of Wellness-Based Greed comes after your loved ones.

For those not familiar with the many New Age tortures out there, who may not be as masochistic or carefree with their funds as I have been, let me demystify a few of these so-called healing practices whose goal is, ultimately, to get you to confess.

## Crainio-Sacral Therapy:

Time to relax? Mais, non! It is time for the Spanish Inquisition! After explaining that the bony plates in your skull are not unlike the tectonic plates beneath the Earth's crust that shift and cram together, causing all manner of upset, the healer cradles your skull and begins to squeeze until you feel like Scarlett O'Hara in *Gone With the Wind* (you know, in that scene where Clark Gable tries to physically squeeze the memory of Ashley Wilkes out of Vivien Leigh's head). While the healer has your head in his Human Vise Grip, he will urge you to confess some dark memory of child abuse or injury (like the time you banged your head on the coffee table when you were six). When you don't confess, the healer rebukes you by sighing and acting generally disappointed, then requests that you come back for another appointment.

### Aromatherapy:

"Smell this eucalyptus," beseeches the pretty aromatherapist. "And this geranium, rose and orange. If you buy these scents and pour them into this $150 diffuser, I promise you will be back in two weeks to tell me how much better you've been feeling." Unfortunately, the only thing I have to confess is that my place smells like a whorehouse in Morocco, and I don't feel better.

### Positive Affirmations:

This is one of the cheaper New Age tortures, which you can do to yourself in the privacy of your own home! All it takes is a book by a New Age guru like Louise Hays, which can be purchased in any New Age bookstore. All you have to do is repeat to yourself a positive affirmation, such as, "Every day in every way I am getting better and better," until all thoughts of unwellness are eclipsed by this one excellent statement. I confess that after a few weeks I feel that "every day in every way I am getting more and more repetitive."

### Pilates:

Strengthen and stretch your body! Lengthen your limbs until they are as lithe as a ballerina's! (Note: read the following with a German accent) "Furst, ve must tie your ankles to ze vooden rack and zen ve vill attach your paws, I mean hands, to ze upper bar ,vere you vill lengthen your spine and contract your abdominal muscles until you *confess*! Name, rank and serial number." All right! I confess! This *hurts*!

**Rolfing:**

"Oh goody, time for a pleasant, relaxing massage," you think as you enter the office of the professional rolfer. No, it is time for the Spanish Inquisition! The next thing you know, the rolfer has jammed his fingers into your joints and is stretching every sinew out of alignment. You feel as though your limbs have been tied to horses about to run in different directions, and the rolfer beseeches you to confess, to cry out, to release any memory that has been lurking inside your tissues. Soon, you will find yourself making stories up, if only this torture will please just stop.

# In Praise of Stomach Flu

The stomach flu is nature's way of telling you that it's time to cleanse your body for spring, so you can fill it with more bad hot dogs, ice cream waffles and beer all summer long!

There's nothing I like better than the cool, refreshing, smooth taste of a cigarette after a gut-wrenching evening spent retching over the toilet. Suddenly, this banal activity that you've been practising twenty times a day for fifteen years becomes once again a virginal experience — refreshing, new, delightful! You would think you had never smoked before! That first cigarette after a good puke takes you right back to your youth, to that very first cigarette you enjoyed in your high-school parking lot — bringing back fond memories of date rape, homophobia and cruelty to animals, along with that wonderful, light-headed feeling that makes you think you should run back into that bathroom and puke again!

Spending three days with your head hanging in the toilet is the closest most of us will ever get to living the life of a glamorous, bulimic supermodel. "Gee, this is really hard," I was thinking, as I imagined myself to be Kate Moss in an effort to ignore the convulsions of my esophagus as it battled the latest vitriolic uprising from my stomach. Whatever those glamorous, bulimic supermodels are making per year — pay 'em double!

When you have the stomach flu, you get to carry a pail around the house with you all the time. Seriously, this pail is a handy thing. It's hard to believe that human beings have evolved this far without the anatomical equivalent of a little pail hanging around our necks. Why weren't human beings born with pouches? You see the great philosophical and scientific questions about mankind that having the stomach flu will bring to mind?

When you have the stomach flu, you can amuse a five-year-old for hours with your sudden ability to belch on command. Really, there seems to be nothing that makes a five-year-old boy laugh harder than a string of really nasty burps bubbling up from a distended stomach that has been starved of solid sustenance for three days. This ability to belch on cue also comes in handy if you feel the need to blow off a telemarketer or blast away a panhandler with the noxious gases emitting from your gullet. If you feel well enough to go out, you can earn the eternal respect of those fat, drunk guys you always see hanging around in bars, who are always up for making a few bucks by holding a good belching contest.

When you have the stomach flu, people avoid you like the plague, thus eliminating that unnecessary personal interaction between individuals that seems to cause so much of the grief and misunderstanding in this world. Fortunately, the stomach flu transforms even the cuddliest of extroverts (even small children) into shivering, evasive misanthropes who cannot bear the sight of another human being, or even a representation of a human personality (like one of those nauseating Muppets) on TV. We should be glad that others disgust us when we are sick, because there is nothing more repellent than someone with the stomach flu who wants to "cuddle". We should be grateful for quivering under sweat-soaked sheets, as it allows each of us to spend precious quality time with our existential and miserable selves.

Think about it. What would you normally be doing? You'd be spending time with existential, miserable friends or relatives, or working at an existential, miserable job — activities that might compel you to go to the local bar with the intent of making yourself nauseous on purpose by drinking several Jägermeisters!

The stomach flu teaches you how to prioritize. When you have the stomach flu, all petty concerns, such as business meetings and the problems of others, melt away into one selfish consideration — making it from bed to bathroom without spilling your guts all over the floor. Life becomes simple, more Zen. You become a walking, breathing example of the rules of karma. Finally you, as an organism, have a singular purpose in life: to never look at what your actions have brought forth again.

When you have the stomach flu, you rediscover your appreciation for the wit and wisdom of Dorothy Parker, realizing that what she said was true: "Spilling your guts really is as unpleasant as it sounds." I imagine it's not too pleasant to read about either. Hot dogs and maple syrup, anyone? Baked beans and melon slices? How about some gin and milk? Popcorn and cigarette butts? How about that new Céline Dion song? (Retch.)

# I Love Animals - They're Delicious

I was seven years old when I first considered becoming a vegetarian. My sister and I were playing in my grandmother's backyard when out from beneath the hedge popped a cute little chicken. Mad with desire to cuddle our fluffy, new best friend, my sister and I chased that chicken around and around my the farmhouse. Each time we completed a lap, my grandmother would say, "Don't chase that chicken, girls! You'll be sorry." Laughing and squealing, we ignored her, chasing the hysterical chicken around in circles until suddenly, for some reason, it decided to lie down and take a nap.

Later that night, as our grandmother dished out the evening's repast, my father turned to my mother and said, "Should we tell them?" At which my point my sister looked at her plate, looked mournfully at me, burst into tears and fled the room. We weren't even teenagers and we had already committed our first murder. Apparently, when frightened, chickens are prone to sudden heart attacks.

While my sister wailed at having her innocence ripped away, I accepted the fact that I was a hardened killer and therefore above bursting into tears. I vowed I would make it up to the chicken by never consuming flesh again. Remorsefully, I ate all the vegetables in a circle around the chicken on my plate — that is, until a little bit of chicken somehow got mixed up with the mashed potato and gravy, and I thought, "Well, I've gone this far, I might as well continue..." and I did, and even though I knew I might go to hell, I licked the plate clean.

I managed to remain painfully thin well into my twenties, thanks to something I like to call the Struggling Writer Vegetarian Diet. This consists of milk, wheat and cheese (the elements required to create Kraft Dinner), rotated with the occasional can of beans. The B vitamins and other nutrients I needed were supplied by copious amounts of draft beer. My carbohydrate-addicted body soon lost its ability to recognize protein as a nutrient, and when I came into a bit of money later in life, I discovered that I had no desire to eat meat at all — just the batter that often surrounded it. My ideal meal was a chocolate shake accompanied by a few shreds of Kentucky Fried animal skin with plenty of gravy — followed by a stiff Scotch.

Then, like Christ, I was reborn at age thirty-three. I woke up one day and realized that I had somehow transformed into a fat, tired, chain-smoking migraine sufferer with crumbling teeth. A trip to the local naturopath confirmed my worst fears. My body, despite its well-fed appearance, was suffering from malnutrition. My liver was a loaf of toxic waste, my blood had an oxygen-deprived ecology similar to the Don River and my intestines were stuffed full of more crap than a serving of haggis. My way out of this dilemma, according to my naturopath, was to "cleanse and rebuild." Cleanse with fruits and rebuild with vegetables. For the second time, I found myself considering becoming a vegetarian.

I considered this as I went to the health food store and paid $14 for a bottle of Extra-Extra-Virgin Cold-Pressed Olive Oil to sprinkle with rice vinegar over my liver-cleansing meal of carrot, burdock and turnips. I considered this as I searched through my cupboards for something real to eat behind the bags of dried, brown dulse and Styrofoam-flavoured rice cakes. I considered this as I sat watching the lid on my $150 pressure cooker rattle over another week's load of brown rice. I considered this as I prepared slimy slabs of tofu with watercress, and as I mixed powdery lumps of kudzu with apple sauce and maple syrup to make a delicious, organic Jell-O. I considered becoming a vegetarian, I really did, until one day, when I was plucking disgusting vegetable nubbins out of my juicer, I realized I had been eating soups that tasted like dishwater and drinking teas that tasted like hot water with a stick of Dentyne in them for over a year, and I hadn't lost weight and didn't feel better. In fact, I felt worse.

I was saved from vegetarianism when I was tested for food sensitivities at Red Paw Data Services. Gleefully, I watched as the results were tabulated — I was allergic to wheat, rye, corn, oats (the staples of the vegetarian diet!) as well as nuts (no more granola!), strawberries, oranges, MSG, saccharine and, gloriously, soy! Soy! No more tasteless tofu slabs! No more expensive, organic, rice and bean microwave dinners or drooly low-fat pudding cups padded with soy protein solids! Feigning an appropriately disappointed face, I asked the technician what on earth I could eat, and she said, "Chicken."

Finally, somebody had given me permission to be a carnivore, and you know what? I feel much, much better.

# P...P...Please Pass the Valium

People are always telling me I should just...relax. "Why are you always so tense?" they ask, in the same slightly patronizing, dulcet tones that Hal used when winding down in *2001: A Space Odyssey*.

"What do you mean by t...t...tense?" I find myself snapping back, accidentally dumping another cup of decaf java down the front of my shirt or lighting a cigarette while I already have one smouldering away in the ashtray. "It's just the w...way I am. I'm a Type-A personality. I...I...I've been this way all my life."

As a child, even the *threat* of an imminent tickle would have me shrieking in terror. Then I would curl up in a ball and cry. The guy who took away my virginity deserves a medal for what he had to put up with, considering that every time he touched me I would slap his hand and run away.

As an adult (well, sort of), I still often find it hard to get hold of myself and can be seen in most social situations clutching my solar plexus as if literally trying to prevent my guts from flying excitedly around the room. This is not because I am nervous, but because my internal organs are so thrilled to be alive they have wings.

I have no explanation for my natural jitteriness, which apparently is so contagious that normally non-drinking, non-smoking people will order a shot and take up smoking again just to get through a meeting with me. I don't know why I'm like this — I was not born a crack baby. Even though I try to explain to concerned observers that flailing my arms enthusiastically while telling a story and accidentally slapping my own glasses off my face is normal behaviour for somebody with my constitution, people still accuse me of being too tense.

My tremors are so bad that I've been accused of being a coke addict, a heroin addict and even of having a hangover a good two years after taking my last drink. Sorry, if I was a heroin addict or hungover full time I might finally achieve that confident, relaxed state of deportment that other people find so amiable and reassuring in a local writer.

Still, I get lots of advice from all kinds of people about how to take the edge off my personality. "Why don't you go home and relax in a nice hot bubble bath?" they suggest merrily, as if taking a bubble bath was the most innocent thing in the world. There is nothing I find more terrifying than the prospect of lying there like Marat in his tub, waiting to have a stroke, as a friend of mine did recently when she decided to take the edge off her personality in exactly the same way. Also, the mind does tend to wander while you're reclining in your allegedly relaxing bath, thinking soothing, Sylvia Plath-type thoughts about women writers being confined to Bellevue and so forth, just for speaking their minds…

People also like to suggest that I relax by taking a nice, long vacation on a sunny beach somewhere far away. What! Are they nuts? That's like telling a vampire to stare at the sun. The last time I went on a vacation — to the Dominican Republic — I found myself trapped in an expensive, fenced-off compound that my travelling companion aptly rechristened "The Prison for Women."

Other over-sensitive, tense individuals have recommended massage as a way to quell my burgeoning ch'i. Now, as someone who automatically responds to any kind of poking or prodding with gales of uncontrollable laughter, naturally I resisted this option for a long time. That is, until I met my present Chinese therapist who, after a few weeks of trying to relax me with a small, curt slap on the rump and the words "Stop giggling!", has resorted to sticking long, shiny, thin acupuncture needles in me to quiet me down. There's nothing like the fear of a needle slipping under your skin, into your bloodstream and maybe eventually piercing your heart, to make you lie still — very, very still.

In the meantime, I've tried breathing in and out of paper bags, walking for two miles every day and smoking a doobie to quell the excess nervous energy that seems to simmer like a brewing volcano beneath my quivering skin.

The paper bag thing works, all right. I did feel slightly more calm and focused, but the problem is, in order for it to be effective, I would have to strap it on my head and wear it all the time, as a horse wears a feedbag. I would be totally relaxed, of course, but the sight of me wheezing through a lunch bag might make other people very nervous.

I don't mind the walking, but quite truthfully, I don't find it very relaxing to trip on the homeless bodies that lie all over the streets. And as for the doobie, well, it just makes me paranoid — paranoid that one day I might have a stroke in the bathtub.

In the meantime, I promise I will try to relax by doing the one thing that seems to simmer me down — watching night after night of awful made-for-TV movies on my 30-inch colour television. What Ritalin is to a hyperactive child, TV is to me. Call it displacement or whatever, but there is nothing I find more calming than watching some screaming, nubile teenage woman being chased around an abandoned warehouse by a machete-wielding serial killer. Now that's what I call Valium for my off-the-Richter-scale soul.

# I'm a Supplement Junkie

I am always looking for a way to enhance my well-being. OK, I'll be honest. I'm a supplement junkie. I gotta have a fix — some kind of vitamin or herb every day — or I fall apart! My hands shake. I can't think. I can't form words. I fear I may go blind! Every day I must get two, three, make that seventeen times the recommended daily amount of phyto-estrogens, phytosomes and bioflavonoids, a special kind of vitamin C, vitamin B drops, echinacea, liquid calcium-magnesium, dong quai, co-enzyme Q, chlorophyll, garlic with wild rosehip, astragalus, blue-green algae, St. John's Wort, gotu-kola, bottled oxygen, sheep's brains, Bach's herbal remedies, or whatever I can get my hands on that is the latest in supplement technology. If there is something that can make me feel good that is not caffeine, alcohol, weed, drugs or nicotine, I will plunk down $20, $30, $130, maybe more, to add it to the collection of feel-good vitamins and herbs on my kitchen shelf. It is the only thing that keeps me from doing windowpane every day for rest of my life! Do you hear me? THE ONLY THING! (Sorry I'm shouting, but I forgot to take my evening primrose oil this morning.)

Some people get a day off, go to the park, spend time with friends, knock back a few beers, maybe go swimming. Me, I spend my time skulking around in the aisles of self-medication meccas, basking in the potential prowess, vitality, invulnerability, superhuman strength and detoxification offered by the rows of pretty little bottles that I can't afford, but which look so nice when lined up on the shelves. So many vitamins and herbs to try, so little time! I spend hours reading the labels of chunky canisters containing freeze-dried powders that promise a full fix of RDAs in one sip and a colon as shiny and pink as a brand new vacuum-cleaner hose. Oh, I don't always go to the same health centre. Sometimes I sneak over to the competitor's shop, where the employees aren't on to me yet. Nothing gives me a thrill so much as peeling the "Sealed for Your Safety" shrink-wrap off a bottle of a brand new, untried substance and finding, beneath the wad of protective cotton, a sparkling city of "dolls" just waiting to take the rollercoaster ride down my throat and speed vital nutrients to my bloodstream.

Let me tell you about the first time I got high. I scored a bottle of niacin, man, not realizing that you don't do niacin; niacin does you. For about five minutes nothing happened. Then I started to feel a bit of nausea. Then my skin started to feel itchy and warm. Then a slightly uncomfortable heat started to spread through my body, making me restless and upset. Next came the head rushes, chattering up the back of my spine and into my skull. Then I saw God. I came down and cried. Don't do niacin alone, man. Do it with a buddy. And never take more than the RDA specified on the side of the bottle.

If you're into downers, you'll really like valerian. It comes in liquid, caplet and tea form. You wait for this pleasant buzz and start thinking things like, "Maybe I shouldn't drive or operate machinery." Soon, everything you touch — even Velcro — feels like velvet on your skin. You know there are dishes to be done, angry boyfriends to fight with, deadlines to be met, but you don't care, man. You are drifting. Sometimes you fall asleep but mostly you just dream. Don't light any cigarettes or candles before you do this stuff — the house could burn down and you wouldn't care.

If you are into uppers, try nature's cocaine, gotu-kola, the berry they used to put in Coca-Cola before they replaced it with sugar and caffeine. I would never take gotu-kola on purpose. I accidentally had some in an orange drink once. I was sitting in front of my computer, working, when suddenly I started seeing little black things out of the corners of my eyes. Then colours became really bright, and my hands started shaking. I had this sudden urge to write an epic poem and run a triathlon at the same time. However, when I got up to start running, my heart started fibrillating like a wounded bird inside my chest. I had to lie down. My life flashed before my eyes several times before I was able to crawl into the shower and rinse the sweat from my much thinner body. Afterward, I could not stop myself from writing "To Do" lists for days.

Sometimes a girl just needs something to help her relax. Sometimes her problem is just merely a case of iron-poor blood. Sometimes she needs a good hit of Floradix — a mixture of iron and B vitamins in (hic) a bottle of alcohol. Or what she might really need is Bach's herbal remedies, a micro-distillation of herbal flower essences in 100 per cent alcohol. A few drops in a glass of water and you have the New Age vodka and tonic. A couple of these and your anxiety just kind of fades away.

# The Twenty-Minute Burnout

Are you ready? Everybody together now...turn the computer on. Great! You're doing great! Now take out your lighter and light that cigarette, light that cigarette, light that cigarette! Good. Very good. Is it lit? Make sure it's lit, or your body won't receive any of the benefits of this warm-up. Now take the cigarette in your right hand and lift it...lift it to your mouth...now hold it there and inhale...two, three, four, and then exhale...two, three, four... inhale, two, three, four...now exhale, two, three, four. This exercise is excellent for toning your triceps and biceps. Can you feel it? Don't worry if you're feeling light-headed. That's how you know the exercise is working. Now do thirty repetitions and switch to your right hand. Inhale, two, three, four...exhale, two, three, four. Do you feel sick? Excellent. That's the oxygen working itself out of your body and being replaced with stimulating carbon monoxide. Now you should be ready to return those unpleasant calls.

This exercise stimulates the vital nicotine-laden force in the fingernails of your right hand as well as important acupuncture points in your right ear. Now punch in those numbers with your index finger. Punch them. Punch them in! It helps if you picture the face of your worst enemy. Let the phone ring. Now scream into the mouthpiece...two, three, four, then pause for response...two, three, four...now scream — c'mon now, let those lazy, irresponsible bastards have it! Tell them what's really on your mind! Let it all out.

Now this time I really want you to make unrealistic, ridiculous demands of the other party...one, two, three, four...pause...now call the other person names. Call them every name you can think of! Let them know you mean business! This is a personal assault! Has the person you have been speaking with hung up yet? Good. Do 30 repetitions, going through all the numbers you have to call. Remember to sigh — wearily, sadly — after each call.

Now you are ready for the advanced-level cigarette and Coca-Cola combination move. If you don't have Coca-Cola you can substitute a cup of coffee with two sugars. Now, pick up the cigarette in your right hand and an open bottle of Coke in the other and smoke, two, three, four. With your left hand, pick up the Coke and chug it down, two, three, four, and smoke, two, three, four, and chug it down, two, three, four. Be careful not to inhale while you're swallowing. Good. Do 30 repetitions.

Now you are ready to open the mail, most of which should be overdue bills. This exercise flexes the muscles in your brow as well as the sobbing mechanism in your vocal cords. Now tear open that envelope and look at the bill, two, three, four, and rip it to shreds, two, three, four. Look at the bill, two, three, four, and rip it to shreds, two, three, four. Now sob to the count of 16. Excellent.

Now kick the trash can. Kick the trash can. Kick. Work those thigh and calf muscles. Remember to switch legs. Now trash your office. Trash it! Take your arm and, using broad movements, sweep everything off your desk. Sweep it off. Push everything on the floor. Work up a sweat! There we go!

Is everything in your office practically destroyed? Good. Now you are ready for some chocolate cake. You need the chocolate cake to keep that precious supply of glucose speeding to your brain. For this exercise you will need some equipment — mainly a fork. Take the chocolate cake and, being careful not to hurt yourself with the equipment, put the cake in your mouth, two, three, four, and chew, two, three, four, and gulp it down. Now repeat. Gulp it down. Gulp it down.

Now look at the heap of work you have to do piled up on the floor. Think of all the commitments, the deadlines, the same old bullshit you have to deal with every day. Now run to the liquor store. Run, run, run. Now get a bottle of scotch, open it and chug, two, three, four, and swallow, two, three, four. Chug, two, three, four, swallow, two, three, four. Now chug the scotch as you run back home. Keep those chins up! Be careful not to spill any! There. Feel better yet? No? You will, after you do this next exercise.

This one will keep you thin and glamorous at all times. Take a needle (make sure it's full of heroin) and inject it into your arm. Yes. That's it. To the count of four…now relax and let your head drop to your chest and then raise it up sharply and look around with a startled expression. Make your eyes really wide. Yes, now…nod, two, three, four and up, two, three, four…nod, two, three, four and up two, three, four. Goooood. Now fall off your chair and lie on the floor. Rest.

We have come to the end of today's workout. There, now, don't you feel completely revitalized and relaxed?

# Martha Stewart Disease

Here are some early warning signs that you may be suffering from "Martha Stewart Disease", as spawned by the unstoppable lifestyle queen.

## Standard Martha Stewart Disease:
• Your house is decorated with your own plaster-cast gremlins and angels.
• Every shoebox and empty tin can in the house has been découpaged with flowers cut out from old wrapping paper.

• You float candles in the punch bowl at parties.
• You use a gold ink pen to sign all your cards and to leave little notes around the house.
• There are pots of herbs on your windowsill, and each is painstakingly labelled with a hand-drawn picture of the herb.
• You've made a doormat with a sunflower design out of old bottle caps.
• Given the choice, you would rather spend your Saturday nights in Home Depot than be taken out for a good dinner.
• You polish your lettuce with a clean white cloth until each leaf shines like a newly waxed car fender before you put it in the bowl.
• You save snowballs from last winter in your fridge, in case you need them to create an ice-sculpture centrepiece.
• You have tie-dyed all of your T-shirts with dyes made from vegetables grown in your garden.
• You've made wind chimes out of old coconut shells.
• Your hedges have all been pruned to resemble chess pieces.
• Your salads consist mainly of nasturtiums and pansies.

## Advanced Martha Stewart Disease:

• Every chunk of cheese on your tray comes with a toothpick and a little flag upon which is clearly labelled the cheese's country of origin.
• Your hair looks like a bonsai tree.
• You hoard cookie cutters in all sizes, shapes and colours in a kitchen drawer, and nobody is allowed to touch them.
• You insist on using ostrich eggs instead of regular-size eggs for the annual Easter egg hunt.
• You put rouge on your children's cheeks so they'll look all fresh and rosy and apple-cheeked when company comes over.
• All of the grass in your front yard is braided.
• You serve entrées in an attractive real bird's nest you found in a nearby forest.
• You make your own Jell-O from calves' hooves rather than buy the powdered stuff.
• You decorate your cakes with ceramic figurines, bundles of chiffon,

buttons, marbles and other inedible stuff just because "it looks so pretty."

• Each and every flower in the backyard is wrapped in raffia and sports a shiny red bow.

• You serve wine to your guests in conch shells.

• You've smeared the walls with yogurt so that, over time, a natural-looking greenish mould will grow, giving your home the fashionably distressed look of an ancient Greek temple.

• You dress all of your children, regardless of gender, in white chiffon dresses and white straw hats with white satin ribbons, and you haven't fed them for days to prevent them from growing into an awkward, gangly phase.

• You've macraméd yourself a computer cozy from hemp and recycled plastic.

• Before you go to bed you spend hours on your hobby farm putting the wool on your sheeps' bodies in hot rollers so they will look more fluffy and glamourous than the neighbour's.

• You sleep outside the house in a tent so that you don't spoil your perfectly made bed.

## Remedies for Martha Stewart Disease:

1) Tie afflicted woman to chair. Brace head with slabs of plywood. Force immovable head to stare at painting of dogs playing poker for one hour first day, two hours second day, three hours third day and so on.

2) A night on the town with Don Cherry and pals.

3) A one-way ticket to Kosovo, East Timor or Rwanda to teach the afflicted woman to appreciate the true meaning of "lifestyle".

# One Out of Four...

# One Out of Four...

It's official. One out of four Canadians is crazy. You know, bonkers. Whoo-whoo-whoo. Ya-ya-ya. Burble-burble-burble.

This is old news to anyone who has ever worked in the film industry or at the post office. I mean, my world was not exactly shattered when I read the headline in the newspaper last Thursday: "One out of four Canadians is mentally ill."

Those of us who work here at *eye* have suspected for some time that the ratio might be higher. In fact, many people I know operate their lives exclusively from the point of view that "Everybody is crazy except for me. I am like the fourth man, the only sane person in a pre-apocalyptic world run amok."

Does anybody else out there find this statistic just the teeniest bit scary? It means that almost everybody in the country, unless they were lucky enough to be an only child, comes from a nuclear family where the odds are that at least one of its members is bonkers.

It also means that in almost any given workplace, someone you work with is suffering from mental illness. The more people you work with, the greater your chances are of encountering someone who wears the sad, clown-like, yet tyrannically thoughtless face of mental illness in one of its many incarnations — depression, paranoia, neurosis, panic, obsessive-compulsiveness, addiction.

In fact, I would venture to say that to suffer from one of these relatively mild disorders, as opposed to, say, schizophrenia or temporal lobe epilepsy, is practically normal.

Now, if you're thinking, "What the heck is she talking about? I haven't noticed anyone acting crazy," or if you were sitting in a room yesterday with three other people and didn't notice any whoo-whoo-whoo, ya-ya-ya, burble-burble-burble going on, chances are that you are that one crazy Canadian out of four that our mental health professionals are referring to.

Since most mental illnesses masquerade as a robust feeling of health and a confidence that everything in the world is going your way, there is only one sure way to tell if you are going crazy — fill out the "Am I Crazy?" quiz below.

## 1.Other people are:
a) to be treated the way like I'd like to be treated.
b) treated for mental illness one-quarter of the time.
c) out to get me...yeah, that's it...they're after me...all of 'em...heh, heh, heh...is that the phone...NO!...don't answer it.

## 2.Love is:
a) like oxygen.
b) never having to say, "Let's live together before we get married."
c) eternal...even if this means I have to kill her, so we can be together forever...heh, heh, heh...because if I can't have her, nobody can!!!

## 3.I wash my hands:
a) before dinner.
b) before performing surgery.
c) with anti-bacterial soap again and again and again because they have been contaminated by viruses like ebola, Lyme disease and God knows what else out there, just lurking on doorknobs and car seats and in telephones...I rub them raw, I rub and rub and rub them until they're clean...sometimes until they...heh, heh, heh...bleed...it's the only way! The only way!!!

## 4.After I eat I:
a) burp.
b) wash my hands again and again to prevent contamination.
c) taste it a second time by throwing up in secret in the bathroom so I don't get big and fat like...heh, heh, heh...Rosie O'Donnell.

## 5.Anne Murray is:
a) a Canadian singer.
b) a Canadian singer who finds it hard not to think of the Bay.

c) an irresistible sex goddess who one day...heh, heh, heh...will be mine, all mine.

## 6.I am afraid of:
a) death.
b) scorpions.
c) clowns...clowns with big red lips laughing at me...everywhere, even, heh, heh, heh, from the pattern in the wallpaper.

## 7.I don't feel I have a drug problem because I:
a) don't do drugs.
b) tried it once and never inhaled.
c) hey, chill out man, heh, heh, heh, what's yer problem...cough, cough...giggle, giggle...snicker, snicker...hey, anybody seen my wallet?

## 8.I get depressed:
a) when something bad happens.
b) after going to a poetry reading.
c) when my plans for complete world domination, heh, heh, heh, fall through.

## 9.I consider alcohol to be:
a) something you dab on an abrasion to disinfect it.
b) the only way to relax my inhibitions so I can get laid.
c) heh, heh, heh, one of the four main food groups.

## 10.I don't get mad, I get:
a) even.
b) a self-help book on how to deal with anger.
c) a machine gun and blow them all away...rat-ta-tat-tat...heh, heh, heh.

## 11.When I look in the mirror I see:
a) a person with an unusual nose.

b) Napoleon Bonaparte.
c) whoo-whoo-whoo, ya-ya-ya, burble-burble-burble, heh, heh, heh.

## 12. The world revolves around:
a) the sun.
b) me.
c) shoplifting, heh, heh, heh.

If you checked even one answer above that contains the phrase "heh, heh, heh" you have gone mad, completely mad, and not in a good way, either. Seek out a health professional, if you can find one that actually acts professional (keeping in mind that the statistics apply to mental health professionals too).

Or ask your employer for one of those "personal" days that everybody seems to be taking lately. You know what those mysterious personal days are really meant for, don't you? Heh, heh, heh. That's right. Whoo-whoo-whoo, ya-ya-ya, burble-burble-burble...

# How to Select a Therapist

I've decided that it's time for me to seek professional help. I want to be normal, dear readers. I really do. I want to give up my sick, twisted ways and walk, talk and think just like you.

So where does one go to seek professional help in Toronto? Last time I sought help for one of my many personal problems, I was diagnosed with the disease du jour, "fibromyalgia", drugged with a tri-cyclic depressant and sent home to gain weight and smile at the chronic abuse in my life. So this time I thought I'd call around and interview the therapist first, to make sure that the "professional" was, you know, to be trusted. However, I soon discovered that most therapists come with a few problems of their own.

The first therapist I called was Dr. P. Aranoia. The conversation went something like this.

Me: Is this Dr. P. Aranoia?
Therapist [*hoarse whisper*]: How did you know to call me...here?
Me: Uh, your number was in the phone book.
Therapist: They must have put it there.
Me: The Ontario Medical Association?
Therapist: No. Who are you? Why are you asking so many questions? Did they send you? How do I know you're not...one of them?
Me: I assure you I'm just a person looking for someone who can help me work out a few personal problems.
Therapist: I have to go. Somebody is following me. [*Click.*]

The next therapist I called was Dr. D.E. Pression.
Me: May I please speak to Dr. Pression?
Therapist [*long sigh*]: What's the point?
Me: The point is that you're a doctor and I need help.
Therapist: Forget about it. When you're dead, nothing will matter.
Me: That's an interesting way of looking at things. How can I make an appointment?
Therapist [*panicking*]: Make an appointment? That means I'll have to get out of bed and go to the office! Maybe you could come over here...
Me [*uncertainly*]: OK.
Therapist: And on your way, perhaps you wouldn't mind stopping at the drug store to pick up some razor blades.
Me [*lying*]: Oops, there goes my other line! [*Click.*]

The third therapist I interviewed was Dr. N.E. Wage.
Therapist: Peace and love throughout the universe...Dr. Wage speaking.
Me: Hi, I'm looking for a therapist and...
Therapist: Halt. It is no coincidence that you called here today. You and I were pig farmers together in 18th-century France, and you killed me because you were jealous of my pigs. I'm afraid you'll never escape me! We are joined together for all eternity!
Me: You mean you're the source of all my problems?

Therapist: Yes, but I can remedy this by placing some crystals on your temples, burning herbs on your solar plexus and anointing you with special oils. Of course, I am not on OHIP and this special therapy will cost you $700. [*Click.*]

I closed my eyes and pointed to a random name: Dr. A.D. Dee.
Me: Hello, is this Dr. Dee?
Therapist: Just a second, there goes my call waiting. [*Click.*] Hello, who is this?
Me: It's me. [*Another click. Seven beeps as therapist tries to dial out while I'm still on the line.*]
Therapist: Hello. How can I help you?
Me: I'd like to make an appointment.
Therapist: Very good. Here we teach people how to communicate. Oops, Just a second...[*seven beeps*]. Hello. Pizza Pizza?
Me: No. I'm on hold.
Therapist [*interested*]: Really? For who?

And then there was Dr. P. Rozac.
Therapist: Good afternoon! Dr. Rozac speaking. How can I help you?
Me: I'd like to make an appointment.
Therapist [*chuckles*]: Oh, that won't be necessary, I'll just write you out a prescription right now!
Me [*shocked*]: Don't you even want to know what my problem is?
Therapist: Problems? There are no problems, only possibilities, and after that more possibilities. [*Starts singing "Don't Worry, Be Happy".*]
Me: Please stop.
Therapist: With every prescription we give you a free coaster with a smiley face on it. [*Click.*]

The next name on my list was a Dr. A. Buse.
Therapist: Buse speaking.
Me: Hi, I'm looking for a therapist.
Therapist: There's no need to be so hostile.
Me: I'm not being hostile.

Therapist: I can tell you your problem right now. You hate men, don't you? Why don't you just admit it?
Me: I don't hate men, I just...
Therapist: Now you're in denial. You hate your father! Admit it.
Me [*sobbing*]: Please stop! I can't take this.
Therapist: And it's obvious you resent authority.
Me: Fuck off. [*Click.*]

# Seven Deadly Ways to Be

Let's see now, there's Greed, Sloth, Envy...um, what are the rest of them? God, these rules are so old I forget! Greed, Sloth, Envy, Bread, Eggs, Milk, Cheese, Broccoli...no, no, that's the shopping list.

Hmmm.

I'd look up the Seven Deadly Sins except there's a cat sitting on the book. Greed, Sloth, Envy...I can't believe I can't recall their names! I mean this is Essential Moral Knowledge! The Golden Rules! I should know this! [*Psst! Think P.E.G.L.A.W.S.* — ed.*]

I'm beginning to get that sinking feeling, you know the one you get when you're sitting in a room of people and everybody's talking about the asshole in the room, but you don't know who the asshole is, and then it dawns on you that it's you! It probably works the same way with the Seven Deadly Sins. The ones you can't remember are probably the ones that you are guilty of! Greed, Sloth, Envy, um...oh, I give up!

Maybe I'm being too hard on myself. Maybe nobody can remember these rules because they're too archaic. For instance, look at Greed. Is that really a sin? Of course everyone's greedy — who can make ends meet nowadays? Isn't Greed just another way of describing the Great North American Work Ethic?

And Sloth? You'd be slothful too if you were a single working mom too tired too clean up after a hard day's work. All you want to do is put the kid to bed and eat potato chips in front of the TV — is that a sin?

Also, if no one can afford to own their own home, you can't blame them for being slothful in the slums in which they are forced to live. What's the use of wasting your energy on projects that never go anywhere? On homes that you can never be proud of because the landlord can't afford to repair them? On jobs that disappear after twelve weeks? On projects that never get any funding? Why age yourself prematurely trying to keep up with the Joneses? That's not slothful, that's smart!

Yep, maybe the old Rules are a little tarnished. Maybe they need a little buffing up so they can gleam again like beacons of morality, beckoning survivors to come forth from the dark, tangled jungle of the evil city and find their way to the Light. At the risk of rending more holes in my already shredded moral fabric, I made a pilgrimage to the Old Wise Guy to ask, "What are the New Seven Deadly Ways to Be?"

## 1.NOT HAVING A LIFE

Very dangerous. Technically, it can mean you're dead. Figuratively speaking, it means you are wandering around wasting everybody else's life and bugging them for clues on how to get one. Often you think that just because you don't have a life, nobody else should either. People with a life see you coming from a mile off, and then your feelings are hurt when they push you away. They can tell you're a vampire! The walking wounded that feeds off the living! You're fucking destructive! Do something quick, but don't try...

## 2.GETTING SOMEONE ELSE'S LIFE AND PRETENDING IT'S YOURS

Often Someone Without a Life finds Someone With a Life who doesn't mind pouring their abundant, generous spirit into the bottomless hole of personal insecurity. These kinds of friendships are based on the cliché that imitation is the sincerest form of flattery. That's why so many wives discard their natural way of expressing themselves to sound exactly like their husbands. Other people who fall into this category are individuals who dress and behave just like their favourite rock star/literary hero/philosopher/you-name-it. You can fool a lot of people by pretending to be someone else for a long time, until the "real" thing pops up and blows you away with integrity. Sooner or later, stealing someone else's act gets you pulled off Life's Stage by the cane of that big MC in the sky. Also, people who pretend to have a life by actually living someone else's eventually tend to turn to the person they're imitating and say, "How can you live like this?" People who find their own way in life would never ask such a stupid, offensive question.

### 3. BELIEVING THERE IS SOMEBODY WHO CAN SHOW YOU THE WAY

People Without a Life invent a kind of human angel/mentor who they believe will just magically appear one day and tell them how to live. Waiting around for this holy individual to show up and solve their problems is a bit like waiting for Godot, but it is a great way to avoid dealing with the big problems like Job, Rent and Love Life.

The problem with people who believe that There Is Somebody Who Can Show You the Way is that they often project wisdom on to individuals who are basically not up for the job — for instance, the bartender or that cute girl riding by on her bicycle. Fact is, nobody is up for the job because the pay's lousy. People who demand to be "shown the way" are often resentful and even more screwed up when they realize they have been led down the Garden Path to a sign that says Dead End by some well-meaning human who has no idea how to help them.

After waiting ten years for the Somebody Who Can Show You the Way, you end up making a wise choice and going to a psychiatrist, who tells you the Way is actually right back where you started.

### 4. RELINQUISHING RESPONSIBILITY FOR YOUR ENTIRE LIFE TO ANOTHER

Some people believe that they are either too wounded or "too much" for themselves to handle, so they place themselves in the hands of someone they perceive to be an authority: a boyfriend, a girlfriend, a psychiatrist, a bartender, a mentor or a family member. They do this by appealing to their caretaker's ego or pocketbook. This is about as smart as offering your neck up to a pair of fangs.

Unfortunately, human beings like nothing better than abusing the power they have over others. It's fun and it sure pumps up the ego. The minute you present yourself to another with that "Handle With Care" sticker stamped on your forehead, no questions asked — what you should really be asking is, "What's in it for the philanthropist?" — is the exact minute you will find yourself smashed to smithereens on the floor of Life's China Shop.

No matter how nice your appointed caretaker is, the fact is you are about as welcome as wet cement on their feet. You're baggage! The old ball and chain! If you relinquish control of your life to someone else, you can't blame them for the bad things that happen to you as a result. If you're hurtin', put a Band-Aid on yourself before someone else decides to operate.

## 5.NOT COMING FROM A DYSFUNCTIONAL FAMILY

If you don't come from a dysfunctional family, then you won't have any excuse for your bad behaviour — so lie and make one up. Incest always arouses a great deal of sympathy. Lying is permissible in the nineties, by the way (or else we'd have no economy).

## 6.BLAMING YOUR LOUSY LIFE ON KARMA

Bad things aren't happening to you because you did something bad last week. Bad things are happening to you either because sometimes bad things just happen or because you made a bad judgment call. Get rational! Get real! Karma, my ass! You're a fuck-up! Learn from your mistakes and do better next time.

## 7.BLAMING YOUR LOUSY LIFE ON FATE

The dog ate my homework, the alarm didn't go off, I had to rescue someone from a burning building on the way and yes, fate did it. It's all fate's fault. Yes, it's easier to believe that you are a tiny little bit of driftwood being tossed around and battered hopelessly by the forces of nature than to ever admit that you are in charge of your own destiny. You can waste a lot of time cursing fate. Why don't you blame someone more specific? Like yourself?

Just don't blame me.

* P.E.G.L.A.W.S.: Pride, Envy, Gluttony, Lust, Avarice, Wrath, Sloth.

# I Want to Suck Your Soul

Vampires. They're real. I know. I'm surrounded by them.

I'm not talking about the kind of creature that sneaks up on you in the middle of the night and leaves bite marks on your neck. No. That's called a lover. We like lovers.

And I'm not talking about those people dressed like vampires who hang around on Queen Street waiting to star in their five-second spot on Citytv. No, those are people with a sense of humour. And we like people with a sense of humour.

I'm talking about "psychic vampires". A psychic vampire is usually someone you know or are slightly acquainted with, who seems harmless yet also seems to have the magical ability to rip a hole in your auric shield, insert an invisible hose into it and drain the very will to live right out of you.

This is the kind of person that you cross the street to avoid because you know that once you enter a conversation with them — even a seemingly innocent conversation like, "How's the weather?" — you'll have to lie down on your bed for an hour to recover.

These people, who seem normal and friendly, have the mysterious ability to tap you like a maple tree. You feel dread at the sight of their often sweetly smiling faces. They have done nothing overtly to harm you, but you know that these people are like black holes into which you find your enthusiasm to walk erect disappearing.

Your personal "psychic vampire" may not manifest in your life as someone you hate. However, you may resent them for making you feel so tired all the time. We're talking about the subtle energies here — the vibes people put out during a personal encounter that somehow go awry and leave you feeling sick or mad — or both — and you don't know why.

I have several psychic vampires that feed off me full-time in real life. One of them is the lady who sells me cigarettes at the corner store. Every day, I go to the corner store to buy a pack of Vantage. Every morning I say, "A pack of Vantage, please." Every day she points to all kinds of different packages of cigarettes, except the brand I have been buying every single day for the last six months, smiles and says, "This one? This one? This one?" I shake my head and point at the Vantage and say, "No, that one. That one. THAT ONE!" until her hand lands on the right package. Then she beams at me sweetly while she collects the money for my cigarettes.

What a psychic vampire may lead you to perceive as forgetfulness or even stupidity is actually a form of passive hostility. A psychic vampire does not bear any responsibility for the relationship, no matter how minor, that they might have with you; they make that responsibility all yours. To quote my old friend Byron Ayanoglu, "When people say sorry, they often really mean 'Fuck You.' "

Then there is the kind of psychic vampire who likes to come off as being the strong, silent type. A lot of contractors, handymen and people who come over to fix your fridge fall into this category. There is nothing more tiring than trying to get important information such as "How much will this cost?" out of a being that is as forthcoming as your basic plank of wood.

You cannot hate this person any more than you could hate a two-by-four, because they have not actually done anything wrong. What they are really doing, however, is silently and perhaps even joyfully feeding off your frustration at their mysterious behaviour.

When work is being done on your home, you might as well leave town. The other option is to stuff your vital life force with breadcrumbs and hand it over on a platter.

Not all psychic vampires feign stupidity or pretend to be deaf mute. Some are actually quite chatty, and you can identify them right away by their manner of speech: "Oh, hi, Donna. And how are we doing today?" The more time the psychic vampire wastes with you on niceties, the more time they have to suction the desire to continue with your day right out of you.

Some psychic vampires also come in the guise of the armchair guru. There can be nothing more draining than listening to a recovering addict or someone who has just returned from a month in Tibet talk about their inner quest. After recently listening to one friend of mine piously go on about his personal empowerment for hours, it dawned on me where these previously disempowered individuals were getting their new zest from — me.

Most psychic vampires feel they are morally superior to everyone else, even though this masks an obsessive need to be clingy. Making their problem your problem is number one on a psychic vampire's agenda. Creating a problem where there is none is number two.

Bunches of garlic, crucifixes and stakes through the heart will not rid you of psychic vampires. The important thing is to identify and avoid them at the first signal they may be subtly working their magic. The symptoms include the inability to focus, stomach cramps, and — when certain people come at you — a frantic urge to run. Let's face it, the body doesn't lie.

The next time you see someone that you've been feeling guilty about because you always pretend you don't see them, let them wave and scream your name, and continue on your merry way.

# World's Biggest Bores

You know how it is. You go to a party to try to meet some interesting people for a change and instead you end up trapped in a corner for hours, listening to the verbal meandering of some insufferable bore who just goes on and on and on ...

I was at just such a party last night and, as luck would have it, I had my tape recorder on. So, at the risk of boring you to tears, I have edited excerpts from my favourite monologues by the World's Biggest Bores:

## Bore Wearing Vintage Tuxedo Jacket and Jeans:
"So you know what my favorite part of *Wayne's World* was? It's the part, you know (laughs), where they're sitting in the car and Mike Myers rolls down the window and says, 'Excuse me, sir. Do you have any Grey Poupon?' That Mike Myers is a genius, man. How about that part where they're (laughs) in the car and that guy who is passed out sings...blah, blah, blah, a fucking genius, blah, blah, blah..."

## Bore Wearing Barbara Kruger T-shirt and Wire Glasses:
"My works use text and fragmented images, codes of meaning appropriated from the self and popular culture to explore the temporal nature of post-modernity in an attempt to address the ambiguity of gender as it has occurred sporadically in instances of patriarchal oppression throughout history...blah, blah, blah, military industrial complex, blah, blah, studied at OCA, blah, blah, unfair granting system, blah..."

## Overweight Bore With Beer in Each Fist and Cigarette Hanging Out of Mouth:
"Yeah. The economy. I just don't know about this economy. A lot of people are hurtin' for sure. Yeah. The economy. This economy is bad. Real bad. Yeah. I haven't had a job for three years. Yeah. The economy. Every time they say this economy is going to get better, it just gets worse. The government is full of liars. Lying about the economy. Yeah...blah, blah, blah, the economy, blah, blah, blah..."

## Expensively Dressed, Constantly Bragging Bore:
"We went down to the Harbourfront readings where we met Daniel. Daniel. Daniel Richler! You know him. He's a good friend. Then we went to the College Street Bar where we ran into

Leonard. Leonard Cohen! Do you know Leonard? Oh. Then we went to a very special private party hosted by Garth. You know, Garth Drab...blah, blah, blah, Moses Znaimer, blah, blah, Atwood is such a good cook, blah, blah, blah..."

### Bore Waiting For Drugs:
"So I phoned this guy at six o'clock and, you know, he's supposed to be here. This guy. He's supposed to be here. Man! You know I've been waiting here since six o' clock. What time is it? Like, I called him at six o'clock and he's supposed to be here! This guy, blah, blah, six o'clock...blah, blah..."

### Bore On The Verge Of Tears:
"So, after I forgave him for sleeping with my best friend, he came back with his friends and broke into my house and robbed me, so I tried to encourage him to go into therapy and he didn't go...so now he's over there ignoring me (choke, sob) after all I've done for him ...he only hit me that once...blah, blah...I love him...blah, blah (choke, sob)."

### Skinny, Long-Haired Bore With Buggy Eyes And Copy Of *The Hobbit* Tucked Under His Arm:
"So, everybody has died from the plague and he's calling out (British accent), 'Bring out yer dead! Bring out yer dead!' And then the guy in the wheelbarrow wakes up and says, 'I'm not dead,' and the other guy says, 'Yes you are!' and then he says 'I am not!' and...blah, blah, blah, Monty Python, blah, blah, 'Bring out yer dead!'...blah, blah..."

### Bore Dressed Like A Vampire:
"I think you actually have to be a vampire to understand what it's like to be the Vampire Lestat...blah, blah...big fan of Anne Rice ...blah, blah...The Hunger...blah, blah...There are vampires living in Toronto. You should be scared...blah, blah..."

### Bore Who's Seen *Natural Born Killers:*

"I mean, I don't know if you picked up on this, because not too many people did — it is quite an exclusive small group of people that actually understand *Natural Born Killers*, but Oliver Stone was manipulating us with his imagery in — listen to me! — much the same way that the media has been manipulating the general public for years. Please cover your mouth when you yawn. I personally watch a lot of films, blah, blah, blah...seen fifty films at the film festival ...blah, blah...Juliette Lewis, blah, significance of blonde wig, blah ...read review in *Time*...blah, blah..."

### Vacuum Cleaner-Collecting Bore:

"Perhaps you'd like to come over and see my collection of antique vacuum cleaners...blah, blah, Electrohome Deluxe, blah, blah, Hoover, blah, blah..."

### Bored Bore:

"God, this party is boring. This city is so boring! Nothing ever happens here. I'm going to move to Vancouver. Aren't you bored? How can you stand living here? Maybe I'll move to Montreal. I'm so bored...blah, blah, boring people, blah blah, bored, blah, blah...Seattle..."

# The Co-Dependent Cab Driver

To me, a taxi ride is not just a taxi ride. It is a metaphor for every relationship I've ever had — an experience that is parallel to the journey you hope to share with that special someone as you travel down life's bumpy Spadina Avenue together, surviving pothole after pothole, no left turns and numerous red lights until you both safely reach your destination.

To me, the taxi driver is the personification of Trust, the person I depend upon for unconditional loving support, the person who will, without harsh words, enable me to reach my goal, my destination, without an ego struggle, an argument over money, or jealousy, because he knows that taking the surest, safest route is the best thing ever for both of us...

Ha! Let's face it. When it comes to choosing Cab Drivers, like life partners, I inevitably make all the wrong choices.

It begins like this. I am standing on a busy street, trying to hail a cab. I want to go east, yet all the taxis travelling east are sending me mixed messages. The light on the hood of the taxi might be on, signifying that the car is not occupied, yet I can plainly see the taxi already has a passenger. This is the Co-Dependent Cab Driver's way of lying to you and also of being a show-off. "We're together and you're not. Ha-ha."

Even more hurtful are the empty cabs that pass right by as if you don't exist, leaving you with a case of low self-esteem. Sometimes a cab actually stops, only to have the driver inform you: "I'm not going your way." All these experiences are comparable to standing around in a singles bar trying to meet men.

Sick of all the lying and cheating, the abandonment and false hope, I am delighted when a cab driver travelling west spies me and does a U-turn. "Finally," I think, as he swerves to the curb. "*I have been chosen. This is the cab driver for me.*" Finally, I can exhale.

Yet no matter how hard I tug, I can't open the rear passenger door. Undaunted, my cab driver, my hero, reaches over the back seat and punches the door open for me. My heart sings! We're together and nothing can stop us now. I get in, and suddenly I am in a toxic relationship. The air inside the cab is perfumed with some vile scent reminiscent of pine, cigarette smoke and the No. 2 Special at the Prince of Rajah restaurant. Indistinct easy listening music bristles through the static from the speakers embedded in the rear dashboard. A pair of dice hang from the rearview mirror.

Without turning his head, he asks, "Where to?" I say, "Queen and Spadina," and he responds, quite sullenly, "Where's that?" It is painfully obvious that the burden of this relationship is to be mine, all mine. I say, "You mean you don't know where Queen and

196 • Donna Lypchuk

Spadina is?" and he replies equally sullenly, "What number on Queen and Spadina?" Like most of the relationships I become involved in, he has already asked me a question that is impossible for anyone to answer. "What route do you want me to take?" he asks helplessly. I tell him to take the shortest, most direct route possible. I want to empower this man by showing that I trust him.

He starts to travel west, away from Queen and Spadina. "What are you doing?" I politely ask. "Taking a shortcut," he says. I ask him to go south and to avoid taking Dundas.

He turns the car around and speeds through a succession of one-way residential streets reminiscent of paths in an Escher drawing. We travel in terse silence, except for the spitting of the radio, down Shaw Street, where he takes a left on to — goddammit — Dundas. After sitting trapped in traffic on Dundas for ten minutes, I can't resist...

"I thought I told you not to take Dundas."

"But Dundas is the fastest way," he whines. "You said you wanted to go on Dundas." He leans over and starts banging his head on the steering wheel — like James Dean. Obviously, the man can't handle any criticism. I am afraid he is going to cry, lose control, suddenly snap and drive us through the wire fence, straight into the Spadding Court Swimming Pool. But what can I do? I need him and he needs me. We are stuck with each other. I must resign myself to the fact that I am the one who will be blamed.

We inch through endless construction toward my destination and the inevitable complete destruction of our relationship. Because the fare is well over what I usually pay for this ride, I have vowed that I WILL NOT TIP HIM...no matter how much he looks like he is going to cry.

The cab finally pulls up to CandyLand, my final destination, and I hand him a $20 bill and ask for three dollars back. He turns around and looks at me helplessly, miming empty pockets. "I don't have any change," he says.

I yell, "Keep it!" and leap out of the cab and slam the broken door because I will pay anything to get away from this horrible, needy, co-dependent man who couldn't wipe his own ass if you gave him a towel!

"You're not the person I thought you were!" I want to scream. Or "You used me!"

Or "You're just like all the rest!"

All I want is a cab driver who will go that extra mile and — even if he is hungry, angry, lonely or tired — can manage an occasional smile. In love, as in cab riding, sometimes it pays to shut the meter off.

# All the Rages

First there was Road Rage. I hope by now that most of you have been fully educated about the disastrous effects that a bad case of Road Rage can have on your health — depression, mood swings, high blood pressure, wife-beating, child-beating, heart attack and, possibly, if you get out of your car and actually shoot the other driver, death.

Here in Toronto we have our own kind of Road Rage — Squeegee Kid Rage. You see it all the time at major intersections: every face inside every car is filled with disgust and a deep, unreasonable resentment toward the starving street urchins with their squeegees and little pails of water. You can feel the communal hatred and the mass desire to just step on the gas and run over one of them "to teach them a lesson".

The lesson we want to teach them is not, "Hey you, don't flutter through the traffic like some fairy from the movie Legend, it's dangerous." No, it's, "Hey, you, don't touch my car."

In our overpopulated society, the car is the last sanctum, the last place that any of us can truly be alone. (Someone else touching my car is like you touching my head when I don't even know you.) Touching my car is like standing too close behind me when I'm trying to withdraw money from the ATM. Touching my car is like looking at my penis when I'm standing at the urinal, fondling my daughter, smelling my mother...flipping the finger at every last dignified, private thing that is left in this society.

So don't touch my car! Don't touch my special, secret fetish, my taboo, my full metal jacket! Would you touch Sylvester Stallone?

Then don't touch my car or me. You touch my car, and I'll get out and beat the shit out of you!

Last week a textbook case of Squeegee Kid Rage was in the news. A man, completely terrorized by the sight of a particularly aggressive Squeegee Kid, got out of his car, confronted the kid and ended up with a split lip. The lesson being: don't ever get out of your car. Stay in your car and repeat to yourself, over and over, "Calm blue ocean. Calm blue ocean. Calm blue ocean," no matter what horror movie is playing itself out across the big screen of your windshield.

Now there are reports out of Los Angeles of a new phenomenon — Rain Rage. A news item on KTLA last week reported that two passersby, apparently driven mad by the endless torrents of rain that have hit the West Coast courtesy of El Niño, landed in the hospital after they beat each other to a pulp. The reason: they passed each other on the street and the edges of their umbrellas touched! Now there's a good reason to kill someone. Psychologists are telling the media that citizens should now watch out for the warning signs of Rain Rage: high blood pressure; inability to let go; red, yelling face; and death. I hope these people aren't thinking of visiting Vancouver any time soon.

Compared to these people, Saddam Hussein looks practically sane. Can you imagine if Saddam was as touchy as your average spoiled, self-indulgent L.A. type? Let's hope El Niño doesn't cause it to rain in Kuwait any time soon.

However, I am worried. There are more than a couple of situations that could lead to the kind of blind rage that could set off World War III if they happened to the wrong world leader.

The touchy situation I am most worried about is Armrest Rage.

You're sitting in a movie theatre. A person sits down beside you and lets you know — just from his breezy, confident manner — that his arm is going to be lying on the armrest, NOT YOURS. The message he is sending you — animal to animal — is that he is the supreme, territorial alpha-human, and you are not. If this was Survival of the Fittest and there was only food for one, he would win, not you. If you were stranded on a rubber raft, you would be thrown to the sharks while he ate the remaining rations.

It is halfway through the movie. Your arm is starting to hurt. Isn't this a shared armrest? Why should he have the armrest? What makes him so much better than you? You try and put your arm on the armrest. The other individual shoves your arm away. But he does it really casually, as if he didn't see your arm trying to settle itself on the armrest. Your only option is to shove his arm away. Then he would shove you. And you would shove him. Then what? That's it. Who does this selfish person think he is? He must be stopped. It is people like this who cause wars! There is nothing left to do but get out your gun and shoot him. Then you must go home and beat the wife, whose eyes remind you of the stranger you just killed. If you're a world leader, you also have the option of pushing the red button.

Let's face it: people are touchy about all kinds of little things.

# The Whore of
# Babble On

# The New Exorcism Rites

Last week, newspapers announced that the Vatican has issued new guidelines to purge Satan from the Possessed. Well it's about time! The last time the exorcism ritual was updated was 1654. No wonder the media refers to Pope John Paul II as "the modern Pope".

Anyhow, I managed to get a hold of the brand-new, leather-bound, 84-page book his hip and hallowed Holiness has retitled Exorcism for Dummies™. That's right! Now you don't have to call in a professional exorcist to drive demons from your loved ones. You can do it from the comfort of your home or car, or even at the office!

Everybody is vexed by demons at one time or another. This handy manual gives you step-by-step instructions about how to proceed with the ritual, including prayers, the sprinkling of holy water and the laying on of hands. The only problem is that the whole thing is written in Latin, that antiquated language nobody speaks any more. The fact that the new ritual is not available in other languages is, however, not supposed to cause a problem.

Cardinal Jorge Medina Estevez, a Vatican official who presented the revisions, was quoted as saying, "An exorcist can use the Latin version tonight if he wants, because the devil understands Latin."

I have some cause for concern that you, the run-o'-the mill freelance exorcist, have no idea what you're saying and may mispronounce certain phrases so that they mean something else — like "Demon, I bid you be exercised" rather than "Demon, I bid you be exorcised," which may cause the Possessed to get up, put on jogging shoes and run around the block. I also find it hard to believe that the devil is smart enough to learn Latin but not savvy enough to pick up the colloquialisms of the culture, which is why I, who studied Atin-Lay in school, have taken it upon myself to translate the new exorcism ritual into modern, plain English that everyone can understand.

Before you begin, you must make sure that the victim is actually possessed by the devil and not suffering from psychiatric illness or

PMS, or just looking for attention. According to the newspapers, signs that a person is under the influence of the devil include "speaking unknown languages and having physical strength disproportionate to a person's age or body." This means that you are free to work the ritual on all unsuspecting foreigners and weight-lifting midgets. Other signs are: mysterious symbols and words appearing spontaneously on the victim's skin; swearing; untoward lust toward inappropriate or reluctant partners; disrespect toward the mother or father; and spontaneously contorting one's body while listening to Ozzy Osbourne. This, of course, means that 90 per cent of today's adolescents are ready for their exorcism tonight. Obviously, there is work to do.

As far as I can discern from trying to decode all the Latin in this new and improved guide, there are two basic ways to get rid of the cloven-hoofed one. The first is the "imploring" method, in which the exorcist basically begs the devil to get out of town. I don't even know why the Pope kept this part in — it must have worked one time when an exorcist said, "Oh, devil, please get out. Pretty please?" and the devil said, "Oh, all right, just because you asked so nicely."

As this nice-guy approach probably won't work, since it is the devil you're dealing with here, I recommend that you go directly to the second, more intense, "imperative" method, which I have translated into everyday English: "Satan, I order you to begone. You are a bad dude. Your presence here has us all deeply bummed." (Sprinkle holy water.) "If you do not get your big red hairy ass out of here, you are going to be in deep shit from the Lord." (If ritual is working, the Possessed should be swearing at you by this point.) "Don't you give me none of your lip, Satan. You can talk to the hand, 'cause the ear ain't listening." (Make "talk to the hand" gesture and sprinkle holy water.) "Satan, you no-good, freeloading bum, we're onto you. You are, as the Pope says, 'a murderer and a cosmic liar.' " (The Possessed should start levitating and vomiting at this point.) "You are co-dependent and in need of therapy. May the force be with you. Obi-Wan Kenobe. The devil is now gone. Make it so. Amen."

This ritual works on the devil, but it may not necessarily work on those possessed by Martha Stewart, Leonardo DiCaprio or Beanie Baby Madness. (Also, sometimes people who are just grumpy or have the flu can mimic the symptoms of demonic possesion.) This ritual has also been known to work on boyfriends who act like they're possessed by Satan but aren't necessarily. Still, the only sure-fire way to get rid of them is saying, "Will you marry me?"

# Deciphering Rent Speak

This week the Necrofiliac has been looking for a new hovel into which to heave her mattress, kitty cats, roommate Geraldo and thirty boxes of biodegradable paper (which she refers to as "My Life's Work" and which the two guys who moved her last time wryly dubbed the "Landfill").

As a result, I have become an expert in decoding the descriptions of potential Home Sweet Homes that appear in the For Rent sections of our local papers. Adjectives and phrases to watch out for are:

**Bachelor: Room for rent.**
**Broadloomed:** What they really mean to say is broad loamed. Stepping on some of the carpeting I've seen is like feeling the springy touch of swamp moss just shortly before it decays into dirt. In fact, I'm not so sure that some of the "carpeting" I've seen isn't actually a kind of green-coloured foam.
**Charming, Eccentric, Funky:** Oh yes, I've always dreamed of living in something that looks like the set from the old Batman series, with crooked walls, slanted floors and ceilings. And yes, that fake wood panelling does look really funky next to that bad sponge job in puce on the kitchen wall. Also, I think the architectural details — those gaping holes in the wall — are really eccentric. It's nice for every room to have a view, even without any windows. And the toilet has a kind of Old World country charm, with its broken handle, pull-chain and brick sitting inside the tank.

**Close to Park:** The space itself lacks a yard or any kind of pleasant access to the outdoors.

**Cozy:** In landlord lingo, cozy does not mean comfortable or quaint. It means tiny and uncomfortable. It means that major fire exits are blocked off every time you open the fridge door. It means you can't open a bureau drawer all the way without bumping the edge of the bed. It means that the kitchen is the bathroom and there's a vanity mirror above the kitchen sink.

**Large:** If it's not large enough to swing a cat in, it's not worth $900.

**One-Bedroom:** Bachelor with a large closet for rent.

**Open Concept:** For those of you who never need to have a moment alone, ever. (Sometimes a creative way to describe a bachelor as a one-bedroom.)

**Patio:** A piece of cement with weeds growing between the cracks, fronted by parking spaces that the landlord has desperately rented out to meet his mortgage payments.

**Plenty of Closet Space:** Ha! Why is it that there are no closets in Toronto? Every single place I looked at has one of those ugly white high-tech rods, the kind that sags so your clothes slide to the middle, fixed somewhere convenient — like in the kitchen, so you can look at the lint on your old winter coat while you eat, or in the hallway, so your guests can be greeted by that vintage ball gown you never wear on their way to the washroom. This shitty hi-tech look is usually accompanied by a couple of crooked wire baskets on castors, so you can trundle your folded sweaters around from room to room — just in case, I guess, you're in the living room, decide to change your top and are too lazy to get up and go to the bedroom. Handy. (By the way, there are a few theories about why Toronto homes have no closets: (a) a closet destroys the look of an "open concept" design; (b) in the olden days, the residents of Hogtown only had one change of clothes, which they hung on hooks on the back of all of those old doors; and (c) straight-laced Old Toronto never built closets for fear that some raving queen might come out of one.)

**Private:** The place has no windows.

**Renovated:** Uh, excuse me, like, renovated when? 1978?

Somebody should tell landlords that just because the place has pot-lighting (with half the bulbs burnt out) or one of those wire garbage-bag holders that folds out under the sink doesn't mean we're fooled into actually thinking the place is renovated.

**Steps to TTC, Park, All Amenities**: That's right, five floors of steps in a building without an elevator. Or just a couple of giant Paul Bunyan steps across the expressway to shops and the lake!

**Studio for Rent**: This one always kills me, especially when they advertise the studio as a two-bedroom that is also broadloomed. I guess you won't mind if I mess up this broadloom with a bit of acrylic paint while I create my latest masterpiece in the studio? Or develop film in the jacuzzi? Or make the second bedroom into a speakeasy? I'm an artist, not a yuppie, you know. If it doesn't have a drain in the centre of the floor, a broken window with cardboard pasted over it and a band rehearsing or a loud domestic dispute in action next door, then it's not a real studio.

**Two-Bedroom**: Usually a one-bedroom in which one of you is expected to sleep in what would normally be used as the living room.

**Two-Bedroom on Two Levels**: Usually the other level is the basement.

# Get the Message?

Last week I tried to return an urgent phone call. To my dismay, an operator's voice came on the line: "I'm sorry but…" So I hung up. I tried the number again. "I'm sorry but…" I hung up again and dialled directory assistance. The number was unpublished. Undaunted, I decided to give it one more try. "I'm sorry, but the fingers you have used to dial are too fast…"

I looked around the room to see if anyone was watching. Fingers too fast? I looked at my fingers. I'd never heard that before. Then I decided to dial the number very slowly. "I'm sorry," said the recording again. "The fingers you have used to dial are too FAT." (Pause.) Oh.

"To obtain a special dialling wand," continued the operator, "please mash your palm to the dial pad now." Completely bewildered, I mashed my palm over the dial pad — and got a dial tone. And what is all that about a special dialling wand? I dialled again and listened again, mystified. Then came the beep.

It was a joke! A-ha ha ha ha. Oh well. In an insecure, halting voice, I left my message. "Uh, if this is the answering machine, please call Donna back." Then I buried my head in my pillow in humiliation.

Yes, I had fallen for someone's stupid answering machine message once again. This one turned out to be a recording lifted from an episode of *The Simpsons*.

More and more, people's outgoing messages function as a kind of creative outlet. Of course, being only human, the more we try to express ourselves, the less often we communicate. A corollary is that the more original we think we are, the more we can rest assured that a huge percentage of the population is leaving the exact same message. These two laws are beautifully illustrated by the following common approaches to the answering machine.

## The Annoying Diarist:

It is one thing to let people know where to reach you during the day. It is quite another to treat your answering machine as a diary. The male version of this sometimes sounds like Martin Sheen in that scene in his hotel room at the beginning of *Apocalypse Now*: "Toronto. Thursday, January 8th. Normal bowel movement. Fine breakfast of orange juice and croissants. I'll be at Kinko's from 9:30 to 10:15. From 10:15 to 10:30 I'll be walking on the street, but I will be checking in for messages from 9 to 5. If this is you-know-who, don't forget to walk the dog."

I have two words for this kind of dweeb — *cell phone*. I also have a question: if you didn't recite this stuff into your answering machine every morning, would your day still actually happen? Would you actually exist? I suspect that you wouldn't, and that that is your greatest fear.

### The Amateur Musician:

We all know this guy. He can play three major chords. So he makes up a song. He thinks he sounds like one of the Barenaked Ladies. But he sounds like thousands of other guys playing their guitar and howling friendly messages into their answering machines right this minute.

### The Drooling 2-Year-Old:

"Ha...ha...hallo? (burble, burble) We...not...what?" (Long painful silence while you're thinking, "Spit it out, kid! I got things to do!") "...oh...home..." Makes you want to send a Hallmark card to the parents that says, "Thank You for Sharing," after you wipe the imaginary drool from your telephone.

### The Psycho Speaks for Me:

This type of person expresses their dark side by taking a famous monologue from a movie and leaving only that on their machine. (My friend Troy once made the mistake of recording Robert De Niro's infamous monologue from *Taxi Driver*. Both his boss and his mother, who were not familiar with the movie, phoned up, heard what they thought was Troy talking about "cleaning up the streets", and began discussing immediate plans for his removal and ultimate committal.)

Another favorite is the monologue that Rutger Hauer recites at the end of *Blade Runner*. If you are very unfortunate, you may even get a bad impression of Humphrey Bogart at the end of *Casablanca*, as in "Hi, this is Humphrey Bogart. So and so isn't home..."

### The Soundtrack of My Life:

The outgoing message can also be a way of subliminally influencing another through carefully selected passages of music. Ah, you play Mozart on your answering machine! You must be a sophisticated, well-educated, sensitive being. Ah! You play Sex Pistols on your answering machine. I better not fuck with you. And who could not help but feel sorry for the poor person who leaves Peggy Lee singing "Is That All There Is?" Then there is the person who tries to convey their mood to you by shouting over a movie theme (Vangelis used to be popular) or New Age music (chanting monks and mad South American drumming are currently all the rage).

## The Minimalist:

This person does not see the answering machine as a tool but actually thinks that he is himself a machine. The minimalist outgoing message invariably sounds like this: "Hi. This is the machine. You know what to do…" It makes me want to leave the message: "Hi. This is Donna. You know what I'm going to say," demonstrating once again how humans naturally use tools of expression to prevent any actual communication from taking place — no matter what.

# The Wonderful World of Office Temping

In the business world there is a natural order. At the top of the food chain is the CEO, then the CEO's kid, the executive secretary, the computer programmer, couriers, the janitor, mollusks, plankton, pond scum and then, finally, the ultimate one-celled animal of the corporate universe: the Office Temp.

The first thing you are required to do when registering with any temping agency is take a typing test. This is where a nice woman who looks like an aging Charlie's Angel takes you to a room and waits while you attempt to duplicate a page from a text on pure mathematics on an old typewriter. After one minute, the woman marks your paper, gives you a little comb and mirror inscribed with the name and phone number of the agency and sends you home to wait for your first assignment.

You find yourself sitting at home, playing with your new comb and mirror for weeks while you wait for the phone to ring. When it finally does, it is almost certain to be at a quarter to eight in the morning after the only night of your life when you decided to dye your hair blue, boff a trapeze artist and swallow the worm in the bottle of mescal. Like a girl scout, however, a good office temp is always prepared, with spectator pumps, navy hose, a crisp white shirt and a navy blue suit ready to go! If not, you can always get away with yesterday's dirty black turtleneck.

Once you have found the building, you inevitably encounter the Woman Who Gives You Dirty Looks. This is the person you will be working with, but you don't find that out until later, because she is incapable of intelligible speech. When you introduce yourself, she is sure to: a) give you a dirty look; b) ignore you; and c) accomplish tasks much more important than informing someone that you have arrived (like separating gold paper clips from silver ones). Once she is satisfied that you have reached a sufficient level of anxiety, this woman, from whom you will also have to procure office supplies, summons the Immediate Supervisor.

The Immediate Supervisor is usually a short, panic-stricken man still wearing the flotation device they gave him to hold his tokens at a recent Club Med holiday. His first task is to change your name. When you say, "Hi, I'm the new office temp," he says, "No! You're late!" After making it clear that the Corporation will not tolerate tardiness, stealing milk from the company fridge or urinary tract infections that necessitate frequent trips to the washroom, the Immediate Supervisor shows you to your cubicle, which, like a mini-insane asylum, is padded in a productivity-inducing bright orange or rainy day gray that makes it difficult for you to hurt yourself or others during your stay. This cubicle often contains a chili-coloured chair missing a wheel, as well as a circa 1981 computer featuring orange letters on a grey background that tell you you might as well commit hara-kiri with your new comb on the spot: Word Perfect 1.0.

After saying things like, "This job requires that we know the alphabet — you have heard of the alphabet, haven't you?" while you nod in acquiescence to the implication that you are such a moron you are lucky to be walking erect, never mind having a job, the Immediate Supervisor leaves.

It is then your job to sit there, sunning yourself under the glimmering fluorescent lights, and dream of the kind of fun $12 an hour can buy. This is also your time to catch a glimpse of the CEO, but this mysterious figure shows himself when you least expect it, like when you are reading old *Time* magazines from the reception area, and asks some impossible-to-answer-question like, "What did you do with my son's guitar pick?" Occasionally, like manna from heaven, a memo or letter for you to retype may appear on your desk. This means it is time for your computer to break down, thus giving you an opportunity to show off your crisis management skills. Sometimes, during such crises, it can take a whole week just to type one memo, and before you know it, it's Friday!

Friday is the most important day in any office temp's career. It is the day when you must get the Woman Who Gives You Dirty Looks to fill out the form that tells the agency how many hours you've worked so you can get paid. Once you have accomplished this step and are satisfied that you have sat enough hours in the cubicle to pay off your most pressing debts, you are ready to complete the final step, which is develop a case of the flu or, better yet, leprosy! Temps' tendency to catch any terminal disease going around is part of the natural order, which is why most office temps are usually killed off by Friday. Perhaps that's where they got their proud moniker: Girl Fridays.

# Kind to Be Cruel

Oprah's show today was about how you as an individual can make this world a better place by performing a random act of kindness. Oprah suggested offering a cup of coffee to the crossing guard at your local intersection, shovelling your neighbour's sidewalk and leaving discount coupons that you don't use on grocery shelves for other shoppers.

Of course, not everybody appreciates being the beneficiary of a random act of kindness (obviously, they suspect your motives), but you can make them appreciate your good will by being gentle and persistent.

## Random Acts of Kindness
## That Could Lead to a Random Killing
### or
## How to Make This World a Better (Bitter?) Place

• The next time you take a taxi, cruise by pedestrians who look like they have a long way to go, lean out the window and offer them a free ride! They'll probably say no, but keep insisting and insisting.
• Tip your bank teller!
• Instead of giving that street person a quarter, give them a great big hug! Remember, affection and good will can be contagious!
• The next time you see someone eating a chocolate bar, offer to put their wrapper in the garbage can for them.
• Compliment people on their appearance by greeting them with "Nice haircut!"
• If you're a secretary, show kindness and understanding; don't just correct those spelling and grammatical errors, take that document back into the boss's office and show him exactly where he made his mistakes! He'll thank you for showing him your wisdom, perhaps even give you a raise.
• Before you leave the streetcar or bus, loudly congratulate the TTC driver for getting you home safely!
• Visit your local hospital emergency room and cheer everyone up by singing songs!
• Next time you're at the dentist, grab a rag and clean out the sink you just spat in. Every little bit helps!
• Give a police officer your phone number and offer to help him crack his next case.
• The next time you see a word misspelled on a menu, pull out that pen and correct it without even being asked!
• Reorganize your girlfriend's purse for her while she's asleep.

• The next time a new band plays, do them a favour by shouting out constructive criticism, such as, "Tuck in your shirt!" It would also be kind to shout out the name of the chord they should be playing, such as "E minor!" Further show your appreciation for the performers by screaming out the name of a more popular band that they sound like, such as "Nirvana!" or "Barenaked Ladies!"

• The next time you see a bicycle courier, compliment his clothing in his own language by saying, "Cool streetgear, dude!"

• Pick the sleep out of a dozing commuter's eye for him or her.

• Discreetly steer an aging friend into the right lighting so that they always look their most attractive.

• Take a lint brush to your local bar and clean the pool table after you use it. A little bit of Windex will polish up that pinball game just fine, too. While you're at it, you might as well clean the toilets.

• Always carry a float of pennies, dimes, quarters and change for $10, $20, $50 and $100 bills so that you are always prepared to make change for others.

• Be kind to small animals. Always carry a roll of dental floss with you to clean their teeth.

• Hang around a high school and offer to escort young teenage boys to the drugstore and instruct them on how to select the condom that is right for their needs.

• Carry a rag with you and polish the chrome on other cars as you go!

• Follow the mailman around the neighbourhood and offer to carry his big, heavy bag for him.

• Before you get in a taxi, spend a little time and draw the cabbie a map (with brightly coloured, scented markers) of exactly where you want to go.

• Bail a stranger out of jail just for the heck of it!

• Make your roommate's day by throwing her bills in the garbage and pretending the mail didn't come.

• Always carry a hand puppet in your pocket to amuse children and distressed adults.

• The next time you're at a restaurant, leave a note inside the menu for the next patron recommending what's good today and what's not,

such as, "Go for the chicken salad!" or "Don't have the veal!"
• Knit booties for cats and dogs.
• The next time you see a woman breast-feeding in public, comfort others who may be embarrassed by walking around the room and stating loudly, "I am not offended. It is a beautiful, natural thing. I am not offended. It is a beautiful, natural thing."
• The next time you're at a crosswalk, let the car have the right of way!
• Pick lint and dandruff off a stranger's shoulder for him.
• The next time someone asks you for a cigarette, say no. Tell him you're doing him a favour.
• The next time you're in a bookstore, save an author time and trouble by autographing copies of his book for him.
• Hang out at the laundromat and offer to fold people's laundry for them.
• Rip advertisements for good jobs out of the paper and, next time you visit McDonald's, present them to the counter person like coupons.
• Write the names of reputable doctors and dentists on the walls of the washroom stalls at your favourite restaurant or bar.
• Amuse people waiting in line by improvising a stand-up comedy routine!
• Help the waitress by helping yourself to that second cup of coffee or beer.
• Phone 411 and tell the operator that you're spending the 60 cents just to say, "Have a nice day."
• Stick little cards with positive affirmations on them on the board at the unemployment office.
• Honesty is the best policy. If a person really is your friend, then he or she will appreciate a heartfelt "You suck!" every now and then. You know what they say — you gotta be cruel to be kind.

# Sadism for Dummies™

Hello, my name is Donna Matrix, and welcome to our seminar, Sadism for Dummies™. I know that most of you wouldn't be here if you didn't feel that you possess certain sadistic tendencies already, but quite often people mistake amateur expressions of resentment, sarcastic remarks and petty ego trips for true sadism. Also, some of you are under the mistaken impression that studying sadism will somehow enable you to acquire riches, glory and fame. But like all healers, sadists use their talents to restore another to a state of wholeness. Sadism is also employed to accelerate the equalization of karma or clarify a muddy situation so that all are humbled before the truly magnificent, amoral workings of nature.

Real sadists use their talents to empower others. They are truly "giving" people. Often they are intellectuals and artists. Quite frankly, I can tell just from looking at your hopeful, power-hungry expressions that many of you would be much more comfortable in my other class, Masochism 101. Only masochists are motivated by martyrdom, greed, self-sabotage or a sense of indignant righteousness. A true sadist would never invite, even subconsciously, retaliation upon his precious being for one minute. So, before we begin, I would like you to fill out the following form, filled with hypothetical situations, so that I can determine your personal sadistic potential.

1.Do you:
a) drink, smoke and have sex?
b) drink and smoke, but have no sex?
c) have sex and smoke?
d) abstain entirely from these vices so you can enjoy the orgasmic pleasures derived from pure sensation?

2.You are a carnie working at an amusement park.Your favourite pastime is:
a) making sarcastic remarks about weird, fat, cross-eyed people wearing Birkenstocks and shorts.
b) ignoring the desperate screams of stranded women and children at the top of the Ferris Wheel while you laugh insanely and smoke Export A's at the bottom.

c) charging innocent bystanders admission for stripping them naked, tying them to the spokes of the Ferris Wheel and setting them on fire.

d) stripping visitors naked and tying them to the Ferris Wheel and setting them on fire for free!

## 3. An appropriate vessel for a pet goldfish would be:

a) a glass fishbowl filled only with water.

b) a glass fishbowl facing a vivid poster of undersea life the fish will never know.

c) an old Galliano bottle so the fish has nowhere to swim but up and down...up and down...up and down.

d) none of the above — you would release it back into the "natural habitat" of Lake Ontario to meet its natural karmic fate.

## 4. It is January 2nd. A person approaches you on the street and exclaims, "Happy New Year!" Your response is:

a) "What's so happy about it?"

b) "The year hasn't happened yet, and I personally haven't experienced it yet, so how can I be available for comment? Make a date in your notebook and contact me in December, at which point I will indeed inform you about whether this has been a happy New Year for me."

c) "Happy New Year! One year closer to the Apocalypse — a time when chaos, plague and fire shall cleanse the Earth of all evil and society as we know it shall be destroyed to make way for a Utopia where people like you and I shall rule the earth — but first all your children must die."

d) "Hey! Oh hi! I'm glad I ran into you. Tonight at my house we have a little get-together planned. Nothing special, just some ritual self-flagellation to  purify ourselves and maybe a little branding to ceremonially mark the passage of the new year."

5.Your favourite celebrity sadist is:
a) Glenn Close.
b) Mickey Rourke.
c) Martha Stewart.
d) Woody Allen.

6.A masochist approaches you on the street and begs, "Hit me!" Your response is to:
a) hit him.
b) make him say please and then hit him.
c) present him with your business card and inform him how much you charge for such services.
d) reply, "No, I will not hit you." When he asks why, you answer, "Because...you want it too much."

**If you answered mostly A's: Delusions of Sadism.** Sorry, you are not the powerful sadist you imagined yourself to be. In fact, your vain imaginings are pathetic and ordinary — the kind of thing that children laugh at on TV. Consider a career in full-time masochism.

**If you answered mostly B's: Beginner-Level Sadist.** You are probably already in some kind of management position at a full-time job you really hate. However, people probably laugh at your painfully outdated, sincere attempts to be scathing, cruel and ironic.

**If you answered mostly C's: Professional Sadist.** Sadly, you have not yet learned the spiritual side of your practice. When you finally learn to be cruel for love and not money, true enlightenment shall be yours.

**If you answered mostly D's: Master-Level Sadist.** You understand the delicate balances that govern the violent forces of nature. You could be a politician, a doctor or a lawyer. You would also make an entertaining parent one day.

# Lessons for Life

Last week, during the teachers' strike, I decided to throw my doors open to the community and let the darling neighbourhood children into my life. They sat cross-legged on my futon, clutching their juice boxes, their big, wide eyes glowing in the light of the Lava Lamp as I wisely passed down the Ancient Truths of My Generation. At the end of the day, I was truly satisfied I had taught them lessons about life that they would never learn in school:

• Never pick anything up off the floor and put it in your mouth without brushing it off first.
• Alpha-Bits cereal does not contain the entire alphabet, so don't waste your time looking.
• The world is not 50 per cent evil and 50 per cent good. The world is 80 per cent evil and 20 per cent good. That's why bad things happen to good people all the time.
• Contrary to what they may tell you, money actually does grow on trees. Where do you think they get the paper they print it on?
• Never run with the scissors pointing toward you. Always run with the scissors pointing outward so the other person gets stabbed and not you.
• The Bible was written by members of the media called the Apostles. Don't believe everything you read.
• By the time it is filtered through the kidneys, human urine is actually a sterile substance. Still, that is no reason to wet the bed and just forget about it.
• Good-looking people are not necessarily trustworthy or intelligent. In fact, they're usually downright evil. Unfortunately, ugly people are sometimes evil, too. I admit this can be confusing.
• Never ever let a fluffy kitten play with Velcro.
• Women who look really young are usually much older than they appear, and women who look really old are usually much younger than they appear. This is the New Law of Nature.

• Never put butter on a burn, in case monsters smell you and eat you for dinner.

• Ambition sucks. Cream rises to the top, but so does scum. Shit floats, too.

• This may be hard to believe, but the United States of America is a Spanish-speaking country.

• It's no big secret how they get the caramel in the Caramilk bar. They get two slabs of chocolate, pour the caramel in between them and sandwich it together with a machine. Big Deal.

• It is OK to pick your nose in public — if you can't breathe. Many people have died from being too polite.

• Human beings did not evolve from the apes; neither were they created by God. We were transported here millions of years ago by Martians, who founded a country called Atlantis, which sank into the sea. Those of us who could swim went to Mexico, Egypt or Ireland, where we founded Civilization as We Know It.

• No good deed goes unpunished, particularly if you are sitting on the board of a charitable arts organization. What's a charitable arts organization? I hope none of you ever are forced to find out.

• You can learn everything you need to know about life by watching re-runs of *Seinfeld* and reading *Allure* magazine.

• In the old days, Sunday used to be a day of rest. Now it is an excellent day to work your butt off to get ahead of the competition! Monday and Tuesday nights are much better times to knock off than Sunday. Don't waste your Sundays lying around!

• Pull-tab tops from Coke cans do not make good wedding rings.

• Jesus did not look like Charlton Heston, Clint Eastwood or Jimmy Stewart. He looked more like Urkel, Bill Cosby or Muhammad Ali.

• Hard to believe, kids, but Sailor Moon is actually Japanese!

• When you grow up and are finally ready to stand on the corner squeegeeing car windows, remember to use vinegar instead of soap. Otherwise, the windows will come out way too streaky.

• A boy dog really is a "son of a bitch".

• Never judge a book by its cover. Wait to hear what Ziggy Lorenc has to say about it first.

• You know you've fallen in love with someone when you start to feel kind of itchy and uncomfortable, you know, down there.

• Working really hard usually gets you more work, but not necessarily more money. Remember, everything in this society is actually designed to prevent you from becoming rich and powerful. There is absolutely no way around this except to scream and scream until you get your way.

• Never put the baby or the poodle in the microwave without poking holes in it first.

• If someone does you wrong and you wait long enough by the river, sooner or later their bodies will come floating by.

• Never let anyone stop you from taking a nap after lunch.

• Money isn't everything. The internet, however, is.

• God is a jolly fat woman who can type 75 w.p.m. and her first name is Karen.